Parker Gillmore

Gun, Rod and Saddle

Personal Experiences

Parker Gillmore

Gun, Rod and Saddle
Personal Experiences

ISBN/EAN: 9783337044237

Printed in Europe, USA, Canada, Australia, Japan

Cover: Foto ©Andreas Hilbeck / pixelio.de

More available books at **www.hansebooks.com**

GUN, ROD, AND SADDLE.

PERSONAL EXPERIENCES.

BY UBIQUE.

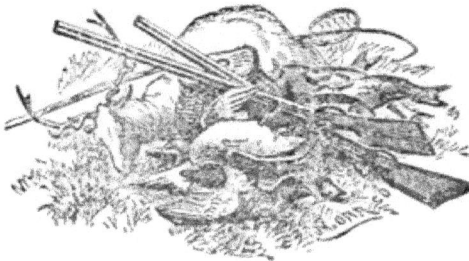

NEW YORK:

W. A. TOWNSEND & ADAMS, PUBLISHERS.

1869.

ALVORD, PRINTER.

ADVERTISEMENT

THE fondness the English gentry have for manly sports is proverbial, and this national taste has the best possible means of encouragement, in the adventurous life necessarily pursued by officers of an army which has its outposts in every part of the globe.

The author of this little volume in the course of his military service had, consequently, the opportunity and exceeding pleasure of indulging in almost every variety of manly sport, the pursuit of which characterizes the accomplished gentleman.

His intellectual tastes led him in early life to the studies of natural history, and his field enjoyments opened wide the arcana of nature—so that he combined within himself the double satisfaction of the true sportsman and the intelligent disciple of nature.

After many years of absence he returned to London, and in the leisure courted after long active service, he prepared for the press the series of sketches which we present to our readers. They were received with great favor on their appearance by the best English and Continental authorities, and in compliance with a very decidedly expressed desire were gathered into a volume

Knowing how constantly increasing is the number of "Sportsmen Naturalists" in the country, this volume is offered as affording refreshing reading and pleasing contrast to the constantly presented sensational literature that now prevails— the publishers believing that there are charms thrilling and healthful in the wild and manly sports associated with the GUN, ROD, AND SADDLE.

The most popular and the most useful of living English naturalists was attracted by these sketches, and upon learning that it was proposed to issue a transatlantic edition, he expressed his approval in the following note:

"I much approve of Mr. Gilmore's book, and should be glad to hear that it is published in America."

FRANK BUCKLAND.

NEW YORK, *March*, 1869.

PREFACE.

HAVING had the honor of holding Commissions under Her Most Gracious Majesty's Flag in two Regiments of the Line, as well as appointments in the Military Train, and in the Commissariat Department, I have, in the course of my professional duties, visited many parts of the world. A natural turn for observation of the habits of wild animals, and a dislike of a wanton destruction of life, has led me to make the best use of my opportunities, whether in the dense forests of Asia, the prairies of North America, the rivers of Japan, the highlands of Morocco, or the vast expanse of the mid-ocean.

On my return to England, I became a contributor to the " Naturalist" and " Fishery" columns of " Land and Water." Permission has been kindly granted to me by the proprietors of that journal to republish my articles. I have, therefore, collected them into one volume, and trust that the now largely increasing class of " Sportsmen Naturalists" will derive benefit and amusement from my stories and adventures with " Gun, Rod, and Saddle."

CONTENTS.

GUN, ROD, AND SADDLE.

WOLF COURSING.

FEW of us have not experienced the excitement
of a gallop over a good grass country, with the
spotted beauties leading the way, getting over the
ground at racing pace, while your mount is nearly
hauling you out of the saddle with enthusiasm and
inclination to make himself on still more familiar
terms with the pack. By Jove, how reckless such
excitement makes you feel! Fear is banished for
the time being—all sense of danger is dispelled to
the winds, and sooner than be thrown out, you
would ride at a canal, or charge any height of
timber. You may be old—yet for the time feel
young: you may be *blasé*—you feel as buoyant as
when you made your *début*. But it is far from
the grass counties, across three thousand miles of
water and fifteen hundred of land—far beyond the

giant Mississippi, to the illimitable prairies of the Far West I wish you to travel, in thought, at least. Imagine an unbounded expanse of undulating land, covered with grass; here and there a sparse scattering of brush, with, perhaps, one or two lines of timber that mark the margin of some tributaries of some mighty river, and you have the landscape without entering into detail. What a place for a gallop! what a place for a buffalo run, or any other kind of run that will give your mettlesome nag an opportunity of showing his pluck and endurance. But take care, don't ride with a slack rein, keep your eyes open; all may look plain sailing from the distance, but on closer inspection you may come upon a densely populated dog-town, or collection of cayotte earths, each hole of which is big enough to use a Newfoundland in for a fox-terrier.

Two varieties of wolves are found numerous all over this elysium; game is abundant, and the marauder is always on its track looking out for the feeble or unfortunate. Skulking scoundrels are these members of the canine fraternity, and cunning withal; keen and successful hunters if necessary, but addicted to idleness; for if they can obtain their dinner at others' expense, they are always ready to sacrifice their principle, and sponge upon the first acquaintance. If you go out for pleasure, or with the desire of replenishing your larder, you are certain to be attended; you can not get away from camp without their watchful eyes detecting you. As you rise one knoll you may observe the escort topping the last, and intently keeping all your movements under their observation. Full well do they know that if buffalo or deer fall before your rifle, on the refuse that you reject, they will find a bounteous repast; or if your hands and eyes forget their cunning, and a wounded unfortunate goes off, then the chances are that the whole carcass will fall to their share, and a gorgeous feast on tidbits ensue, for master Lupus has wonderful scenting powers, and, with the trail spiced with blood, he grudges no amount of exertion.

Again, the wolf is always in disgrace; he steals your game if deserted for a few hours to procure assistance to transport it to camp; he eats your lariat ropes, untying your animals, nibbles the flaps of your saddles, and keeps up an unearthly serenade through those hours that the tired sportsman is most disposed to rest in. Is it any wonder that

he is unpopular, that he has no friends, and that he
is considered a vermin of the first magnitude? The
American wolf, although divided into many families,
those we have to do with are the large gray species,
and the cayote or prairie variety, the former of
whom is a large, ill-looking savage, the latter less
repulsive, seldom over twenty-three inches at the
shoulder, with more of the dog in his physiognomy,
and a good deal of the fox in his nature. In all
shooting excursions you will have idle days, a lay
off for the more serious duties of the morrow, when
guns are cleaned, bullets cast, powder flasks re-
plenished, and wet or dirty clothes dried or washed.
The forenoon having sufficed to perform these labors,
a run with a wolf will be found not a bad appetizer
for your evening meal, or remover of your little
stiffnesses and ailments, in the same way as a little
exercise is necessary to the hunter the day after a
long or hard run. To enjoy this pleasure to perfection you must be provided with dogs, and there are
none so suitable as the strongest stamp of greyhounds; more powerful ones that are addicted to
grappling with the foe will get fearfully mauled, for
the jaws of a wolf are almost as powerful as a
hyena's, and consequently your limited establish-

ment would be half the time on the sick list; with
the greyhound it is different. As soon as you get a
view, at him they go, and although the game is
swift, still his adversaries are not long in ranging
alongside, when a snap in the hams or loins immediately brings him to bay. Determined and numerous are his efforts to catch the nimble antagonists,
who take precious good care to keep beyond reach.
After a few moments of such skirmishing, the closer
approach of the sportsman admonishes the wolf to
be moving, and off he goes, best foot foremost; but
his persecutors are in attendance. A hundred or two
yards may be traversed, and again he is brought
up standing from a similar cause; thus the game is
played till the wolf is exhausted, and the sportsman
gets sufficiently close to end the episode by a well-
directed pistol-bullet through the grizzly marauder's
cranium.

Spearing the wolf on horseback is also capital
sport; but it takes a great deal out of your nag,
for the scoundrel, while fresh, will double almost as
sharply as a hare, and from his wonderful lasting
powers takes you over an immense distance, he
invariably choosing the roughest ground. In this
mode, also, you must constantly be on the *qui vive*,

for if opportunity offers he will make either your horse or yourself acquainted with his grinders, and a snap from him will be a memento. In the neighborhood of Fort Riley an accident of this kind almost occurred to me. A large gray wolf jumped up before me, and as my horse was fresh, and the afternoon cool, I made up my mind for a run. Drawing my revolver, and taking my nag in hand, we were soon skimming the prairie at a slashing pace. After a mile of this work, I ranged along-side, but on several occasions, when about to press the trigger, the wolf wheeled sharply to the right or left, once very nearly throwing my nag on his head. More determined to draw blood from the trick practised on me, I was soon again at his tail; but the foe tried a new and quite unexpected ruse, viz., suddenly slackening his pace, and as I overshot him, making a most wicked snap at my off foot, which fortunately was protected by a heavy cowhide boot; but the indentation showed that a lighter foot covering would have caused me to regret my prowess.

If ever you visit the Western Prairies you will not regret the trouble of taking with you some good strong greyhounds; the rough Scotch dog I should prefer, for you will not only find them great promoters of your sport, wolf-hunting, but useful auxiliaries in pulling down wounded deer, as well as most watchful and trustworthy camp guardians and companions.

SHARKS JUMPING AT FOOD.

In "Land and Water," a correspondent who has
been yachting during the summer, mentions the
circumstance of a leg of mutton being lost which
was hung over the side, and two blue sharks afterward making their appearance; doubtless they
were there before the meat disappeared, and had an
active part in its disappearance. When cruising in
the fore-and-aft schooner " Sunny South," on the Mosquito Coast, a few years since, the steward hung a
roast of beef from one of the stern windows, and to
his annoyance it was *non est* in the morning. The
weather at the time was very calm, and it was consequently supposed that some forecastle hands had
got down in the rudder chains and appropriated it,
although how it was to be cooked without discovery
was difficult to know. However, a second piece was
about being hung out, which doubtless was to be
well watched, when, as the piece of line was about to
be made fast, a violent pull was felt, and on the

steward running out his head to find the thief, it
was found to be a shark instead of a man; the fish
had sprung at least three feet from the water to
secure his prize. A friend of mine, while fishing
with a deep sea-line, was nearly losing his hand
through one of these blood-thirsty prowlers of the
deep. The fish had not been biting rapidly, and
careless from want of success, the hand in which he
held the line was outside the gunwale of the boat
and close to the surface; fortunately, he happened
to cast his eye at the moment overboard, and just in
time, for a shark, seven or eight feet long, was close
to the surface, coming straight for it. On examining
the head of a shark, it will be seen that from the
position of the eyes, they can well see what is taking
place above them, and in all instances where I have
observed them take a bait, they always got underneath before seizing, turning on their side at the
moment of laying hold. I never previously, till
reading Mr. Buckland's remarks, saw it stated that
a shark scented his prey; nevertheless, I have long
thought so, and that their olfactory nerves are of the
greatest acuteness and use in directing them to
where it is to be found. On two occasions, once in
the Southern Indian Ocean, on another, off the north

coast of South America, near Los Rocas, although
no sharks had been seen previously, they appeared
about the ship soon after some of the most venturous
had bathed. Again, I was on board a vessel becalmed, within sight of the volcanic rocks, St. Paul's
and New Amsterdam. The captain kindly lent his
gig to myself and companions to procure some specimens of Cape pigeons, Cape hens, and albatross. A
great number of birds were killed, and whether it
was the scent of blood or not, I can not say, but a
white shark about ten feet long joined us, and
remained by us till our return to the ship. He was
afterward caught by using a Cape hen for bait.
On examining the head of a shark, the snout will be
found to project a long way over the upper jaw, and
although there are no regular nostrils defined, such
as will be found in the salmon or trout, there are
a great number of minute orifices, doubtless intended
for smelling, and which duty I am inclined to believe
they most ably perform.

SEAL PRESERVE.

NOVELTIES are universally run after, but who will try to adopt the following? True, it is not in the power of many; still some have the facilities. We have deer parks, pheasant covers, grouse moors, and rabbit warrens; still we have no seal preserve. I can fancy I see Mr. Frank Buckland looking aghast at the proposal, and exclaiming emphatically, "What! Give a home and protection to the destroyers of my darling children *Salmo salar?* Such a proceeding would be worse than sacrilege, and all the other abominable crimes known, taken collectively and jumbled up into one heap." Within easy ride of San Francisco, the capital of California, is situated the Ocean House—a great resort, in warm weather and holidays, of the *élite* of this prosperous Pacific city, for here at all times a fresh breeze can be inhaled, and, excepting during a calm, the grandest, largest waves seen, lashing with impetuous fury the precipitous towering cliffs of a wild, iron-bound coast. Close to the Ocean House are some rocks, and on these at all hours can be beheld numbers of seals. The Legislature of the State has, I believe, passed an Act for their protection, and so well does Master Phocæ know his safety, that I doubt if he would not dispute possession of his demesne with any representative of *genus homo* that had the temerity to intrude. The Californians are very proud of these pets, and well may they be, for they form a strange and most interesting picture, reclining in all attitudes, young and old, big and little, free from fear and happy in their security. Many of them have been named from some fancied resemblance to persons. One, the king in stature, and most savage and repulsive in physiognomy, bears the *sobriquet* of Benjamin Butler, of New Orleans notoriety. An old resident informed me that he remembers this veteran seal for years, and that his countenance was a good index of his temper. At night, from the Ocean House, you can constantly hear them bellowing, and old Butler's voice, from its depth and volume, is easily distinguished from the others. I expect that San Francisco for many years to come will be the only city that possesses a preserve of pet seals.

OYSTER CULTURE.

WITH much pleasure, both in the United States and in England since my return, I have read a number of most interesting communications from Mr. Frank Buckland, H. B. M. Commissioner of Fisheries, and others in reference to oyster culture. It has long struck me that not nearly enough attention was paid by my fellow-countrymen to this unbounded field of operations and wealth, and if they still continue to neglect their opportunities after the ability and energy with which the columns of "Land and Water" have pointed out the means of prosecuting the good work, let the onus lay on their own shoulders, for truly they deserve it. It is a well-known adage, "that one man can take a horse to water, but an un-limited number can not make him drink;" the horse might not be thirsty, and there are excuses for his refusal. But dear Old England, with her immense population, is always hungry, and has always mouths to feed, and I feel certain that with the amount of

admirable coast that our island-home has, this description of food, which is both wholesome and nutritious, could with due attention become so cheap that
it would be within the reach of both rich and poor.
I do not for a moment profess to an excess of
knowledge; but while sojourning in North America,
where oyster culture has been studied and practically
tested for many years, the experience of some of the
most capable persons in various sections of that
country I learned, and they·unanimously agreed with
what I have so lately seen stated in your columns,
that a warm summer is the great desideratum for a
productive deposit of spat. In fact, I can see no
other feasible reasons to be advanced by our transatlantic cousins for their well-known success than
that the warm waters of the Gulf Stream run along
their coast, and that they have intense, almost tropical, heat in summer—such, in fact, as we have had
during the past season.

Your accounts unanimously agree that your de-
posits of spat have been most abundant this year;
but if the heat should be less the coming one, and
should the produce only be one-half, I am still convinced that the returns would be far more than
sufficient to indemnify the outlay; however, if a

difference of opinion should exist, the experiment is worth trying, which, if successful, forget not to give the praise to whom it is due. Of course a great number of our fellow-countrymen know the United States; some of those may have taken interest in this subject, and possibly are better informed than I am; still there must be a great mass that know nothing about the American oyster; to those, then, I will give the benefit of my experience. From Massachusetts to Florida, with more or less abundance, oyster fisheries have been established, not only for dredging, but for cultivating. The result is, that this delicacy can be obtained at moderate charges even in the interior towns and cities, such as St. Louis and Chicago; in fact, there is scarcely a respectable *table d'hôte* eastward of the Mississippi, on whose bill of fare they are not to be found. In the Dominion, where the winters are proverbially severe, they are equally abundant; New Brunswick, Nova Scotia, Prince Edward Island, and the estuary of the St. Lawrence, have long proved themselves prolific in this respect; corroborative of the fact that if you can get heat, such as we annually have, it does not matter how severe the winter may prove, for the abundant reproduction of these bivalves.

2

It has struck me that the American oyster may be of a different species from the English ; the shape is not the same, and the flavor (possibly many will say this is prejudice) I think, if possible, finer. If they are, could not the home-bred species be benefited by introducing the stranger? Experiment would soon elucidate this, for the American, if packed with the hollow side of the shell down, in solid masses, can be kept alive for months; in fact I have been shown them thus stowed away in cellars, when they had been built in over ten weeks ; what, then, would a voyage of ten days, under such circumstances, signify? The motion of the vessel might shake out some of their moisture (on which they subsist), but certainly not all.

The pinna fisheries of the Mediterranean some years ago used to be most abundant; from want of culture and the improvements in dredging machinery, it has lately sadly deteriorated, almost to nil. In enlightened England don't let us follow the example of the improvident natives of Southern Europe, who, so long as they can obtain the dinner of the day, care not and think not where to-morrow's is to come from.

AMERICAN PARTRIDGE.

(ORTEX VIRGINIENSIS.)

IF all our countrymen who have traveled abroad or sojourned in foreign lands had done so with their eyes shut, or if not keeping their orbits closed had refused to give their countrymen the benefit of their experience, a useless lot they would have been, and England, as far as progression is concerned, would have been far behind her present advanced position. He who first introduced the idea of crossing our native horse with the foreigner, did an immense public service; he who introduced the old Spanish pointer, deserves the gratitude of every sportsman, for doubtless our present beauties, with all their speed and sagacity, have much of the blear-eyed, bad-tempered, pottering old scoundrels' blood in their veins; and still further, to foreign climes we trace the pheasant, the turkey, and so many more valuable animals, that to enumerate them would be tedious. However, I believe that there are quadrupeds, birds, and fishes, still strangers to our land, who but require to be known to be appreciated; and by placing the merits of any of them before the public, some one may be found sufficiently patriotic to make the attempt to naturalize them.

Without more preamble, and to come at once to the point, let me say that in my humble opinion there is no bird more worthy of attention, and more deserving of the honor of introduction to our preserves, than the Virginian partridge, often misnamed in America quail. His numerous good qualities, together with his description, I will to the best of my knowledge give, hoping it may be the means of yet seeing this little beauty ornamenting our fields, and adding brilliancy and variety to the game-bags of our numerous enthusiastic sportsmen. The American partridge varies in weight from eight to ten ounces, is erect in his walk, very handsome in plumage, strong upon the wing, feeds principally upon grain, grass-seed, and ants, frequents indifferently brush, timber, or open country, is capable of standing great cold, is not quarrelsome with other game, is very prolific, frequently hatching two broods in a season Moreover, an advantage which can not be too highly estimated, is that it never gets so wild as to rise so far from your dogs as to be out of gun-shot, a nuisance that all are so well aware of in our home-bred bird toward the end of the season. In fact, who that shoots regularly can not remember instances of our partridge disappearing over the far side of a field as soon as the sportsman had entered it? Now, in years of experience in America, I never saw an instance of this kind; up to the commencement of the close season they would remain almost as tame as they were at the termination of the previous one. A reason for this may be that they seldom pack; only once or twice have I seen more than the usual number of a covey together, and then remarked that the weather had been unusually severe and stormy.

A peculiarity, however, this bird possesses is that in wet and slushy weather he will frequently, when disturbed, take shelter on the limbs of trees, from where, if flushed, they afford the hardest possible shots. This bird in the open is by no means easy to hit, for his flight is very strong and swift, and frequently irregular, but he does not go far, so that a good marker seldom has much trouble to refind him. Some persons are under the impression that this partridge is migratory; however, this is a mistake, for although they may wander from their breeding place, from constant attention, I am convinced that the change of quarters is caused from scarcity of food. On the edges of the dry prairies in southern Illinois, in early autumn, this bird abounds; in winter they disappear into the neighboring thickets and brush, for why? the prairies are constantly burned at the end of the season, and consequently starvation or change of residence is their alternatives. In one section of the country that I resided in, a great portion of the prairie land was too wet to burn, and many a heavy bag I obtained late in the season, even when the roots of the grass were submerged in ice. My dogs, which I invariably broke upon them, seldom made mistakes, and never do I remember a covey departing (except the pointer or setter had run into them coming down wind) without getting at least a barrel into them. I believe these birds are equally adapted for naturalization into either England, Scotland, or Ireland, and with other varieties of game they appear to agree well, for I have on several occasions killed this partridge with one barrel, and the ruffed grouse with the other over the same point.

As a table delicacy I know no greater; for weeks

I have constantly had them at both breakfast and dinner, still without becoming satiated, and there are very few varieties of game could stand a more severe test. Their note or call is remarkably melodious, and in the spring or pairing time, when they are numerous, you can hear their sweet voice all day long, and in every direction. I have always regretted that no one has thought of introducing this little stranger, and nothing could afford me greater pleasure than to be the medium, for I feel perfectly confident that neither would ever have occasion for regret.

AQUATIC HARE..

In one of your late numbers allusion is made to a
tailless hare. Of course, any new or but slightly
known animals, their habits and modes of life, are
subjects of great interest to both the naturalist and
the sportsman; permit me, therefore, to call your
attention to an aquatic member of the *Lepus* family,
with whom I became acquainted during my sojourn
in North America. A little before sunset, on a fine
calm evening in March, I took my stand upon a
bridge crossing a slough in the southern portion of
Illinois, with the hope of killing a few wild ducks.
The atmosphere was so clear and still that the birds
were very late in visiting their feeding grounds.
While impatiently trying to kill time, I saw something swimming in the water, and supposing it to be
a common American musk-rat, and being desirous
of a new tobacco pouch, I stealthily stole along the
margin of the water, well hid in the flags, to
endeavor to obtain a closer shot, for the musk-rat

requires a tremendous deal of killing. However, having knocked over my game, in a few minutes my retriever laid it at my feet; but imagine my surprise when, instead of a rat, I found it to be a hare. I could scarcely believe my senses, but seeing is believing. Of course, I thought that the poor creature had been driven to water to avoid a foe; but before many days I shot several, and all in similar situations. The habits of this new variety I now made a study, and found that they were amphibious, sleeping in form on the edge of the morass during the heat of the day, and feeding, before sunrise and after sunset, on the different descriptions of water plants. Whether this hare was able to dive or not I did not ascertain, but that he is a most expert swimmer there can be no doubt. His size is the same as that of our common wild rabbit, but from his build being thicker he may possibly be heavier. His legs are short, feet large, ears small, and head very full and round; color dark-grayish brown, with scarcely any white upon the scut, and the fur exceedingly soft and fine. I frequently tested his qualities on the table, and can speak in the highest approval of the delicacy and delicious flavor of his flesh, which is much lighter in

2*

shade than that of any other of the same family with
whom I am acquainted. The skin, which is very
thin, is easily removed from the carcase; but great
care must be taken to prevent it getting torn. On
inquiring, I found that this hare was well known by
the squatters, and from them learned that it bred
only once a year, generally producing two at a
birth; and that the young at a very early age
follow their mother in her sundry aquatic excursions
in search of the delicate water plants that form their
staple food.

SALMON IN JAPAN.

(SALMO SALAR.)

No person, I am certain no gentleman, ever disputes the nobility of the salmon; he is an universal favorite with all, whether they be disciples of Isaac Walton or believers in Dr. Johnson's interpretation of the word "fisherman." As this noble fish is so universally popular, it may not be without interest to many of the readers of "Gun, Rod, and Saddle," to know that he is more universally scattered over this world than is generally supposed, and that he is a highly appreciated article of food, and of great commercial value, in countries so far distant from our island home that we may almost with safety call him a cosmopolitan of the northern hemisphere.

That the salmon was found in abundance in all rivers in America, from the Hudson River, New York, northward, all probably are aware; that he

is extremely numerous in those rivers that flow
north through the Hudson Bay territory, into the
ice-bound Arctic seas, less are cognizant; but that
he perfectly swarms in the streams and estuaries of
the North Pacific Ocean, many, I am certain, are
ignorant. Yet he does swarm in those distant
waters, until lately only known to whalers and
fur traders, in such countless multitudes, that their
arrival is looked forward to from season to season
as the great event of the year—for with his coming,
privations from hunger terminate, and an abundance
of nutritious food is not only temporarily secured,
but a hoard laid up sufficient to last through the
protracted term of a rigorous northern winter.

When traveling in Japan, what was my delight
to hear that salmon were numerous in these favored
islands! Naturally I looked forward with avidity
to the hope that I might be so situated as to obtain
a day's fishing on the margin of one of its distant
rivers; however, in this I was disappointed, but
nevertheless had the fortune to make acquaintance
with an intelligent Japanese merchant, who not only
showed me numerous specimens of the genuine
Salmo salar, but gave me abundant information
regarding their habits, and the method there pursued

for their capture. From observation, inquiry, and research, I am inclined to believe that the salmon, whether in the Atlantic or Pacific, seldom approaches nearer the Equator than the forty-first or forty-second degree of north latitude. On the Atlantic sea-board of the State of New York, the Hudson River formerly was his southern limit; but alas, that stream is now totally deserted by these valuable visitors, the result of weirs, or the indiscriminate pollution of the stream with the *débris* of saw-mills, chemical filth from manufactories, &c. On the eastern shores of the Pacific the same parallel will be found the southern boundary of this fish; while on the coast of Japan, Tartary, and Siberia, his haunts are marked by the same line of demarkation.

From the exclusive laws of the Japanese Government, I was unable to travel farther to the north than Yeddo, except it were to visit the port of Hakodadi, and consequently was prevented from obtaining a personal knowledge of the homes and resorts of the salmon; for although they are brought in immense numbers into the latter town for sale, they are not captured in the immediate vicinity. The Japanese salmon that I examined resembled more those on the Tay, in Scotland, from their

excessive depth and thickness in proportion to their
length. Their average weight appeared to be about
twelve or fourteen pounds, yet several I saw would
have turned the scales at thirty. The color of the
skin was in all less brilliant than in our home
acquaintances, possibly the result of transportation,
the method of curing, or the shade and consistency
of the water out of which they had been taken.
However, the flesh was undeniably excellent, and
brilliant in hue, and in no way inferior to those
from our most appreciated rivers.

From my informant I found that the habits of
their fish were identical with ours, and that so great
were their numbers that they formed the staple
article of food for the poorer residents of the
northern portion of the Japanese archipelago; that
they were captured principally by stake nets, set
in the fluvial portion of the rivers; and that the
English method of taking them with a fly (which I
explained) was entirely unknown. As I could not
have the honor of being the first of my countrymen to capture a Japanese salmon in the legitimate
sportsman's method, I may have had the honor of
tying the first artificial flies that ever were cast on a
Japanese river; for so interested was my listener—

and the Japanese are wonderfully intelligent, totally the reverse of the self-conceited, pig-headed China-man—that I dressed a couple of what I considered the most killing specimens, and which he promised to use, as instructed, on the first available oppor-tunity.

An intelligent Russian officer whom I some months afterward met at Tien-tsing, in Northern China, and who had been for years stationed on the Pacific, gave me the most glowing account of the immense quantities of salmon that frequented the Amoor River and its tributaries, and his information perfectly tallied with that obtained from my Japanese friend. Now the mouth of this river, and the north-ern portion of the Japan group of islands, are in about the same latitude, and are only separated by about three or four hundred miles of sea, showing that most perfect credence might be given to both informants.

Fifty years ago, who would have thought of Englishmen going to Norway to fish? Possibly, as the world grows older, with the rapid strides of improvement in machinery and transportation, we may hear of fishing parties being organized for Japan and Siberia, and, in addition to the numerous

splendid specimens of *Salmo salar* that now decorate
Mr. Buckland's museum, we will see numerous
beauties that once parted with their silver sides the
blue waters of the Pacific.

WILD-FOWL SHOOTING.

In my protracted rambles about the world, I know no portion where this sport can be more thoroughly enjoyed than in America. I have always been passionately fond of wild-fowl shooting, and the bags that I have made in the United States and Canada have far exceeded those obtained elsewhere. As wild fowl are nearly all migratory by inclination, or are compelled to be so from the changes of the seasons, it is of great importance that you should visit the various haunts at the proper periods of the year. However, the rule is, for successfully carrying on war against the web-footed families, go north in summer and south in winter. In June, July, and August, the wild-rice fields of the numerous labyrinth of lakes of Minnesota and the north-west territory, perfectly swarm with wild fowl, while in December and January they will be found equally numerous on the large bayous and lagoons that surround the mouth of the Mississippi. Of course, in the intermediate portion of country between Minnesota and the Gulf of Mexico, during the seasons of migration, splendid days' shooting can be obtained; but the stay of the birds is so short that it would not compensate for a special visit. Where thousands are to be seen to-day, not a dozen will be met to-morrow; but if you should happen in the spring and autumn to be in either of the States of Illinois, Iowa, or Indiana, when the frost and ice are breaking up in spring, or when winter makes its first appearance, you may with safety calculate on having some of the finest sport. A year or two since, when in Illinois in November, a sudden change took place in the weather, and although the morning was ushered in mild and warm, by noon it was snowing, with a gale of wind blowing from the north. From experience I knew that such a day was not to be wasted over the fire. I got on my shooting-ground with a very large supply of ammunition, and in two or three hours had to cease, as my stock was exhausted. My stand was in a field of Indian corn that had been gathered into shocks, from the back of one of which I took shelter from the blast as well as concealment. Never shall I forget the scene. The ducks came in thousands, all flying before the wind, and if a dozen guns had been there instead of one, abundant work would have been found for all. On another occasion, in the same locality, two friends of mine killed, in two or three hours in the evening, and in an hour and a half the succeeding morning, eighty-four wild geese and thirty brace of mallard duck. In the spring of 1866, when in Iowa, the first day of thaw, I went for a stroll, scarcely expecting to find game; but when I got on the prairie land, I was perfectly astonished at the clouds of wild-fowl arriving from the South, some of the ponds being so densely covered with duck that the surface could scarcely be seen. These birds were all coming from the South, where they had passed the winter. If any of my readers intend to go in for work, and not object to roughing it, I should most decidedly say that the wild-fowl shooting is good enough to justify a Western visit; but let him not be induced to keep in the vicinity of settlements; but let him and his attendants commence housekeeping on the margin of one of the northern Minnesota lakes, if in summer (remember one that produces an abundance of wild rice); but if the reverse season should be selected, the southern tributaries of the Mississippi will afford him abundant sport, and any of the hospitable Southern planters will deem it a favor if you will do them the honor of making their home yours.

SHOOTING IN BARBARY.

THERE are a great number of gentlemen in England who can spare the time but not the money to rent, at the present fabulous prices, shooting at home. For the benefit of such I will state that capital shooting can be obtained at Tangiers, and that the expense of going and returning, including a stay of a month, need not exceed forty pounds. Gibraltar, your first stopping-place, can be reached by one of the Peninsular and Oriental steamships from Southampton, or by one of the numerous Mediterranean steamships sailing from Liverpool. The passage money by the former, to go and return, would be about twenty pounds, by the latter fifteen. From Gibraltar, feluccas almost daily cross to Tangiers— twice a week formerly, and probably still a steamboat with cattle does the same. The fare for this portion of the journey should not exceed a couple of dollars, and a good hotel will be found on arrival, where I have resided, at the rate of one dollar per diem. Safely established under the guardianship of the hostess, you can obtain all desirable information, and a guide if such you deem necessary. An hour's ride from the town, going inland, will bring you upon splendid ground, either scrubby brushwood, covered slopes, or open grass and palmetto plains. The game principally found is red-legged partridge, which, contrary to our home experience of the same gentleman, here lays well to a dog. Hares are also plentiful, snipe, plover, and the lesser bustard not uncommon. Just beyond Cape Spartel there is a small river on which I have killed a great number of duck, and a mile or two farther on an immense swamp, known by the name of "the Lagoona," where snipe and wild-fowl may be killed in abundance, as well as woodcock and wild-boar. As the gates of Tangier are always locked at sunset, you have to hurry home at an inconveniently early hour, but if you do not object to roughing it, and prefer a long day and large bag to the luxury of a well-aired bed and comfortable apartment, you can easily arrange so as to sleep at one of the numerous Arab villages or douàrs. Of course, to do this, you will require an interpreter, who should also perform both functions of cook and major-domo. But to one in-

convenience you will have to submit, viz., fleas.
They may not be the largest in the world, but for
numbers and bloodthirsty proclivities I will back
them against any others. The Moors are a fine,
manly, handsome race, and invariably sportsmen.
To a proficient with the gun they soon attach themselves. Sometimes I have been followed for hours
by some of them, and a clever double shot would
always elicit their admiration. However, there are
some ugly stories in circulation of shipwrecked sailors
and adventurous Europeans having received any
thing but a hearty welcome; but this is directly in
contradiction to my experience, for day after day,
alone, I shot amongst them, and frequently slept in
their villages with no other attendant than a youth
from the hotel at Tangiers, and their conduct was
uniformly kind and courteous. The weather also is
delightful in autumn, and the country extremely
pretty, while all around the town are abundant ob-
jects worthy of a visit on your idle days. In fact,
I have little hesitation in predicting that the first
visit will most probably not be the last.

THE STRIPED BASS.

THIS fish is known the entire length of the sea-board of the United States, and is almost as popular as the salmon. There are many reasons for this; he is game in the highest sense of the word, fighting with the most determined obstinacy as long as his strength will permit, frequents alike the ocean tide-way or river, taking generally with avidity the greatest varieties of natural and artificial baits, and ultimately being fit food for the most fastidious epicure. By naturalists he is placed among the perch, and has been named *Perka Labrax*, an indignity which he is in no way deserving, for he is built on the beautiful lines of the salmon, possibly with a little more depth and beam, and his coloring has a nearer approach to that of the lordly *Salmo salar*, save that horizontally along his sides are placed several lines (generally seven) from the gills to the tail, and from which he doubtless derives his familiar name. Early in April, if the weather be favorable, this fish

makes his appearance in the rivers *en route* to their
spawning beds (from this date he becomes the object of attention to the pot-hunter, for I can not call
the man who tries to capture fish in that state by
the name of fisherman), where he remains for some
time, probably over a couple of months. This duty
performed, they return again to the coast, affording
sport for a short period, then disappear to return in
September and October in immense numbers, glad-
dening with their advent the heart of every sportsman.

Their size is so varied that they may be taken
from the weight of a few ounces up to sixty and
even more pounds, the heavier fish generally being
captured late in the season; and woe betide the
angler if unprepared he should strike his hook into
one of the leviathans, for all his fishing paraphernalia will certainly receive so severe a shock as to
render it for after use completely worthless, that is,
the portion that is left with him. After spawning
this fish does not lose its condition like the salmon,
therefore his capture immediately subsequent is not
nearly so reprehensible, the propagation of his
species not injuring him to a noticeable extent,
therefore, if he be fished for in the rivers after that

3

duty is performed, nothing is so attractive for his capture as a gaudy sea-trout fly; but the striped bass is not dainty, and many persons of experience persistently use with the greatest success a piece of white or scarlet rag tied over their hook instead of the more complicated and expensive invention. Fishing in the sea, however, the shrimp is the most popular and gentlemanly bait, trolled along the surface after the manner of the fly, at which the fish break, similar to trout or salmon; still there are days when you can not thus allure them; and soft-shell crab, spearing (a small transparent fish about the size of a minnow), or squid, have to be resorted to; even the spoon bait has been known to be successful when all other attractions have failed.

Although this fish annually chooses a change from salt to fresh water, still it is not necessary for his existence, numbers having been experimented on by detaining them for years in fresh, where instead of losing flesh, they were pronounced to have improved much both in size and condition. So exceedingly popular is the striped bass in America, that those watering-places in whose vicinity he is known to abound, receive annually an immense influx of visitors attracted chiefly by the prospect of enjoying this fishing. Even a club-house has been built, and a very large association formed of the principal gentlemen in and about New York, who spend a great portion of their summer vacation at this retreat, and as I have been informed by many of the members (some of them salmon fishermen of experience), that the sport they there have is only second to what they could obtain on Labrador or Canadian salmon-rivers.

I believe that this fish could be most easily intro-duced to our waters, and that he is well deserving of the effort, for he is very hardy, and I do not think so likely to be affected by the pollution that so many of our streams suffer from; they also appear to be immensely prolific, for traffic, netting, drain-age, &c., may have reduced their numbers, still they are to be found in great abundance even in such crowded water-thoroughfares as the Bay of New York, Hudson and East rivers, that any person duly initiated in the necessary mysteries can, at the proper seasons, confidently expect a heavy basket as a reward for his trouble, and that within sight of the numerous spires, store-houses, and busy thorough-fares of their handsome western metropolis.

Great and unprecedented trouble has been lately

taken successfully to introduce salmon and trout to the southern hemisphere; with how much less difficulty could this fish be transported here; no tropic to cross, only one fourth or fifth the distance to traverse, and steamships to be found sailing almost every day of the week. Certainly this matter is worthy of consideration, for not only would thousands find amusement and health in their capture, but a wholesome and excellent article of food be provided for our immense population.

SHOOTING IN CHINA.

"You may go to Hong Kong." This name is frequently substituted for another place currently supposed to be warmer, but at the same time in close proximity, for the soldiers used to say, on whose authority I know not, that there was only a sheet of brown paper between the two. However this may be, Hong Kong is a very warm residence during the southern monsoon, for the high hills that protect the back of the garrison at that season shut out every breath of air. For all this I never saw the thermometer over 98 deg. Fah. in the shade, so that according to statements of some of the late residents at Wimbledon, England in tropical heat can successfully compete with the world. But if the weather should be warm in this distant portion of Her Majesty's dominions during one portion of the year, the temperature is delightful when the northern monsoon sets in, and out-door amusements can by change be the more appreciated. The

characteristic features of this island are a succession
of mountain peaks, in parts very rocky and barren,
the balance of the hill-sides being covered with
stunted brush. However, there are two valleys
tolerably well covered with timber, viz., the Happy
Valley and Taytan Valley; in the former is the
race-course, where annually is held a meeting, also
the grave-yard, where worn-out man is deposited.
A pretty spot is the Happy Valley. The name, I
think, not inappropriate, when we remember that
it is the place of assembly, where crowds meet to
enjoy the equine contests, or where man is laid to
rest from all the troubles and annoyances of this
life when he has run his worldly course. The
quantity of game to be found in the island is very
limited, and consists of a few hog-deer, a few
pheasants, some partridge (much resembling the
black partridge of India), and at certain seasons
quail and snipe; but the results are most uncertain,
and half-a-dozen birds, all told, will be deemed a
successful day's work. But if Hong Kong does
not afford many inducements for the lover of the
double-barrel, the adjacent mainland, when you are
acquainted with the localities, does; and if the
reader will have patience, I will endeavor to give

a sketch of an expedition, and the ground visited. Fancy yourself on a rattan-built wharf running into the harbor from the godowns at the back of the Danish consulate, a handsome lorcha of about sixty tons, taut-hauled up to her anchor, waiting impatiently a hundred yards from the shore for the moment of departure, while two or three sampans are incessantly plying back and forth, loaded with guns, dogs, portmanteaus, and good things for the inward man, ranging over the interval that exists between *pâté de foie gras* and Madame Cliquot. At last the finishing load is delivered, time is up, the blue-peter is hoisted at the fore, and at the instructions of our kind-hearted host, we descend into his gig, and are rapidly on board the larger craft. The wind, which is fresh, just suits; a few turns on the somewhat primitive capstan trips the anchor, and shaking out the immense mainsail, her head is pointed for the Cap-shee-moon Pass, the great high-road of traffic between Hong Kong and Canton.

As we leave the labyrinth of shipping and junks of every nationality and shape, and draw farther clear of the land, our speed increases to eight knots. The pass reached, two or three tacks have to be

made, when we stand direct for Castle Peak Bay,
our destination; and what a pretty spot it is,
sheltered from the cold winds: both grass and
shrubs grow in luxuriance down to the edge of
the water, while at the head of the bay is situated
one of those quaint joss-houses, of architecture pe-
culiarly Chinese, imbedded in a grove of banyans.
The country around is a succession of rolling hills,
gradually gaining height as they recede from the
bay till they reach an elevated rocky ridge of most
irregular outline, one portion resembling an old
castellated ruin, from which, doubtless, this placid
bay gains its name. When within a hundred yards
of shore, "let go the anchor" was given, and we
swung round and surveyed our shooting-ground
with satisfaction expressed on every countenance.
The day before our party started, information had
been brought by a cooly that the quail, in their
regular autumnal migratory flight, had arrived; and
scarcely had we progressed inland a hundred paces
before the dogs were standing, and from that
moment, till dark, the time for loading was even
grudged; the quantity that we brought to bag I
forget, and consequently fear to make a statement;
but this I know, it far exceeded our most sanguine

expectations. The country around here appears at no late date to have been cultivated; but whether the peaceful tillers of the soil had desisted on account of the neighborhood having obtained a very bad reputation for piracy I know not, but our experience in England tells us how fond these little migratory beauties are of haunts that the plow has ceased to turn up. Next morning our range took us farther inland, the quail still were abundant; but as we got to the upper ranges, where a dwarf palmetto flourishes, the Chinese partridge was found. This bird has a very strong resemblance to the black partridge of India in plumage, but exceeds it in size; never is found in coveys, and lies extremely close to a dog. Time after time I have walked up to a point, quartered my ground, or headed my dog; still no bird was visible; believing it to be a false alarm, I have been on the point of giving up the search, when whirr, the wily bird would rise, and go off like a thunderbolt. In all my experience, I know no other whose flushing makes such a commotion, or whose flight is so rapid.

This bird is not very abundant, and is called by the Chinese Cha-coo, doubtless from its note, which much resembles these two syllables when whistled.

3*

Four or five brace of them in a mixed bag is considered extra luck; still I have killed within the space of two hundred yards three couple, each bird flushing singly and apart. About midday we reached a Chinese village, imbedded in trees, with a considerable cover lying backward from it. After lunch we beat it, and three splendid pheasants were our reward. The pheasant of southern China is truly a regal bird in comparison with our home-bred introduction. They weigh one-half more, and their flight is so rapid, that if the sportsman, in a cross shot, does not shoot well ahead, his game bag will long be kept ignorant of their weight and dimensions. Two or three times during the day I was frightfully fooled. The dogs were standing stiff as a fence-rail, and, of course, something extra was justly expected, when, what do you think? a bird that feeds on snakes and lizards, lumbering in flight, and of gross plumage, was flushed. In the south of China, this species is known as the crow pheasant, his size and long tail having doubtlessly gained the latter portion of the appellation; but on inspection, no one can help wondering at the indignity the bird of Colchis has suffered in having such a brute bear his patronymic. For my own part, I

think this filthy-feeding bird is of the jay family.
During this day's work, several painted quails were
bagged—a truly beautiful little bird, smaller than
his namesake, but swift on the wing, and more
delicate, if possible, on the table. Still they are so
small, and the brilliant feathers so delicately pencil-
ed, that I never cease to consider their death as an
unnecessary slaughter.

Time flies on rapid wing; I had only three days'
leave of absence, so that one day more was only
left; duck and snipe shooting I have always had
a passion for, so when we arose in the morning,
not much refreshed with sleep (for the cowardly
Chinese coolies kept constantly sounding the alarm
of Lally-lunes—*anglice*, pirates—which kept turning
out the whole party, revolver in hand), we determined to devote our last day to this sport. A wide
expanse of distant marsh and paddy fields was our
beat, and well it was that such a decision was come
to, for we truly had some splendid shooting. Several
ducks, a host of bitterns of every size and color, and
innumerable snipes, composed our bag, the painted
variety of the latter being very numerous. Although
this is a handsome bird in appearance, he is sadly
behind the common snipe in sporting requisites,

being heavy and slow of flight, seldom wild, and
very inferior for the table. That night we beat
back to Hong Kong harbor, while the stentorian
lungs of one of the party, and the key-bugle notes
of another, awoke the slumbering echoes of the
neighboring hills, and astonished the celestial seamen, who passed on their various missions, with
what "all that bobbery could be."

Castle Peak, from what I have said, can easily be
found by any of the sportsmen at the distant garrison of Hong Kong; but there are numerous other
shooting-grounds as good, and scarcely farther distant, viz., the Shangmoon Valley, at the top of
Pirates' Bay, the covers at the top of which always
harbor pheasants; the far side of Meer's Bay, after
crossing the Kowloone Ridge, have afforded me
many days' excellent sport; and the nearest end of
Llama Island to Victoria, about two or three hours'
sail from the Barracks, if occasionally visited, will
yield ample remuneration for a few hours' work.

DUCK SHOOTING IN AMERICA.

It may not be uninteresting to sportsmen to have an account of what sport they may look forward to if chance or intention should place them on the prairies of the Western Continent. It has long been my belief that Nature had strongly before her the wants of the votaries of field sports when this favored land was constructed, for the abundance of indigenous food, the variety of cover, the distribution of water, and the salubrity of the climate are such, that probably in no other portion of the globe similar happy combinations can be found; and, as a result, the abundance of game falls not one iota behind what might be expected. In wild-fowl shooting there are two desiderata on which success depends : first, suitable weather; secondly, the gunner being clothed in suitable colors. Having both the above advantages, please to imagine yourselves, on a cold, blustering afternoon, a few flakes of snow falling, and a strong presentiment of a severe frost before morning, situated among the withered leaves of a persimmon bush, on the edge of an interminable slough, in the center of one of the western prairies. In every direction that you cast your eyes, ducks will be seen, flock upon flock, while single birds, like an army of skirmishers, dart here, there, and everywhere. Having arranged your shot, powder, caps, and loading-stick, as most convenient—that is, provided you shoot with the muzzle-loader, and I am still old-fashioned enough to believe it the hardest hitter—for every moment is of value, look out; you will not be kept long waiting ere such work commences as you seldom or never previously enjoyed. Your situation, half up to your knees in slush and water, may not be conducive to health, but all the inconvenience is more than overbalanced by the excitement of the moment; and what will not a man endure, if possessed with true sporting proclivities, to gratify his passion, and does he not consider himself more than rewarded by the possession of a heavy bag, alike evidence of his skill and hardihood.

On the afternoon of November ——, I started for my blind; the weather was such as clearly foretold the sport to be anticipated. My hardy mustang soon brought me to the scene of operations, and,

after attending to his creature comforts, I was stationed in my blind, a few corn-stalks and grass
having been added to the withered foliage of the
bush I had selected, the better to screen me; further,
I had tied a bunch of prairie grass around my cap,
to assimilate it more to the color of the cheerless
landscape; at my feet was an old and true friend, a
setter, whose perfections in the hunting-field, or
retrieving by water I never saw excelled. At first
the sport was but languid, only an occasional duck
passing within range, so that after an hour only four
or five mallards had been brought to bag, but as the
day advanced and the weather became more inclem-
ent, I had less leisure to ruminate and take note of the
passage of time. By four, P. M., the ball had opened
in earnest; if I had had two guns and an attendant
to load, still they would not have been idle. First
come half a dozen mallards sweeping along in front
of the blast, the pace terrific; about forty yards off
they pass to the left; with intuitive knowledge the
gun comes to the shoulder and eye, and at the correct
moment the triggers are pressed; good two yards in
front have I to shoot, and my judgment is correct,
for a bird topples over to each report, while the sur-
vivors rush upward with unaltered speed, take a

sweep round to find from whence comes the danger, and, disliking the neighborhood, start for parts unknown and less to be dreaded.

As I hastily sent home my wads over my shot, keeping an eye all the time to windward, what is that ever-changing cloud I see, reminding one of the reflected light that glances off the backs of a flight of gray plovers? By Jove, they are blue-winged teal! On, on they come, occasionally rising or swooping downward as fancy directs. In a moment they will be here—for your life don't move; even depress your eyes so that the rim of your hat will prevent the leaders seeing them. At last they are within range, and each barrel's course is marked by a lane of birds, whom the shot has caused to alter their forward movement. As night approaches, the pintail and butter ducks put in an appearance, and without cessation your gun plays its part, the pile of game at your feet is becoming enormous, and Beau is never idle for a moment. As darkness increases, you think of going home, still linger for one or two more shots. Now you can only see the birds on the wing that are between your sight and some clear spot in the sky, but around you on the water are thousands. As every arrival is greeted

with a loud quack, quack, frequently so close at
hand that you start, almost believing that one of
your victims has come to life. But hark! what is
that honk! honk! Geese! I can't go till I dust
some of their jackets. As none of all the web-
footed tribe are so wary, extra precaution is
necessary. At length you see a massive dark line
against the sole clear portion of northern sky
remaining. Would that heavier shot were in my
gun. Onward they come, slowly and cautiously;
waiting till they are nearly perpendicular, I play
my part, and the heavy splash on one side and
thud on the other clearly states that two are down,
one in the water and the other on shore. With
such a finale you cease, nor is it too soon, for I
really believe that if you were to remain after darkness you might receive an injury, as the birds, no
longer dreading a foe, rush about in the most reckless way, that I have felt quite a relief at getting
out of the marsh without a mallard going at express
speed coming in contact with my cranium. On the
night in question twenty-eight brace of ducks, two
geese, and three brant was the bag—good sport, as
all must agree, for three or four hours' shooting.

RUFFED GROUSE.

(TETRAO UMBELLUS.)

In "Land and Water" of May 30th, I have advocated the introduction into England of the American partridge (*Ortex Virginiensis*), having perfect confidence in their being most suitable birds for naturalization, knowing them to be almost perfection in sporting qualities, and very superior as additions to the larder; but with all my partiality for that little beauty, I will presume upon your space and good-nature by mentioning the claims of one of the grouse family, that equally deserves honorable notice and the attention of those persons who may be desirous of having a greater variety of feathered game than at present is to be found. The ruffed grouse (*Tetrao umbellus*) must not, however, be confused with the pinnated grouse (*Tetrao cupido*), for although both have a great similarity in appearance and size, their modes of life and choice of quarters are totally dissimilar, the former being found among timber or brush, or in its immediate vicinity, while the latter chooses the open grass-covered prairies, perching upon trees only when the winter is very severe and the ground covered with snow, and then making use of such trees as are always to be found standing alone, and sparsely sprinkled along the margin of these immense western savannas. Both these varieties are splendid birds, but the characteristics of the ruffed grouse make him much better adapted for a residence here, and so strongly am I disposed in their favor, that I believe if once introduced they would as soon as known outrival the pheasant in popularity, being much hardier, swifter on the wing, lying better to dogs, disinclined to run before flushing, requiring the quickest and straightest aim to bring them to bag, nor are they much inferior to the oriental favorite in beauty of plumage.

The ruffed grouse a little exceeds the red grouse in size, being almost eighteen inches in length, is very handsome and upright in form, of a beautiful rich chestnut-brown color, variegated with gray and dark spots, and pencilings on the back, breast, and neck. The tail is gray, with a black bar across it near its termination, and is generally carried open like a fan. On the top of the head there is a slight crest, and down each side of the neck are curious fan-shaped tufts of glossy, black, velvet-looking feathers. In April these birds pair, but I should imagine from the seasons in the northern portion of the United States and Canada being more backward than ours, if they were introduced here they would do so a month earlier. They lay from ten to sixteen eggs, their nest, which is a very primitive one, being generally secreted in brush or under the shelter of a fallen log. They are most affectionate parents, and use the same artifices as the wild duck to draw away the intruders from the vicinity of their youthful progeny. This grouse has two distinct calls, one a soft, mellow, prolonged note, generally used in gathering after the covey has been broken up; the other an extraordinary drumming sound made by the cocks in pairing season, and capable of being heard in still weather a great distance. The latter noise is caused by the rapid vibration of the wings when the male is perched on a fallen tree or stump. Indiscriminately they live on a great variety of food—ants, grubs, alder-berries, wild cherries, and grain being their favorite diet. Early

in autumn, when the weather is fine, particularly in
the morning and evening, they will be found in the
open cultivation, more especially if there be rough
ground with brush in the vicinity; but as severe
weather approaches the woods will become their
constant resort. In shooting the ruffed grouse,
great difficulty is always experienced in marking
them. The flight, as I have previously said, is
wonderfully rapid, and they have a method of
doubling back in the reverse direction in which
they started; however, as they do not generally
go far (about three or four hundred yards), with
patience, and a selection of the nearest irregular
ground which has young timber upon it, or the
densest brush that is in the vicinity, a second
opportunity will probably be again found of bringing more of the family to bag. All over the United
States and Canada they are to be found, being
generally known by the misnomers of partridge and
pheasant. Where the country is wide and sparsely
settled, they are sometimes stupidly tame, almost
permitting themselves to be knocked down with a
stick. Frequently, when trout-fishing in the wilds
of the State of Maine, I have come suddenly upon
them, when they would rise into the nearest tree,

and remain with unconcern watching you, when, from evident curiosity, they would stretch their necks, and get into all kinds of grotesque attitudes, and so little would they then regard the report of a gun, that I have known pot-hunters kill quite a number of the same family by always shooting the lowest birds first. But when the ruffed grouse becomes familiar with man, he is perfectly cognizant of the danger of being in his proximity, for although they lie close enough to shoot at, their color harmonizes so well with that of the ground that it is next to impossible to see them before they are on the wing, when such is their impetuosity that the timid, nervous, pottering shot, or the poacher with all his devices, would find it next to impossible to kill a single specimen.

In the undergrowth which springs up in that portion of the country where the timber has been destroyed by fire, in the States of Maine, New Hampshire, and Vermont, I found them very abundant, it being almost impossible to wander half a mile from camp or settlement without flushing a covey. Now the winters here are particularly long and rigorous, far exceeding in severity those of Scotland; still, the bird's natural hardiness prevents his suffering. In the Alleghanies and all the southern ranges of hills

of the United States he is also abundant, where, if
the winters are less severe, the heat in summer is
sometimes excessive, proving that the ruffed grouse
is capable of enduring great varieties of climate.
The palate of the most fastidious epicure can not fail
to be gratified with his appearance on the table, the
flesh being extremely delicate, with a strong flavor
of our red grouse. I have eaten them cooked in
every conceivable manner, and whether it be simply
roasted over a camp fire or forming a portion of an
omnium-gatherum stew, they will be found alike
acceptable. Although scarcity of food may compel
this grouse to change his beat, still they are not migratory, as stated by some naturalists. This supposition has arisen from their being found in great
numbers during summer and autumn on the scrub
barren land, which they leave as soon as the more
severe weather commences, for the shelter of the
dense timber. A family of these birds I was acquainted with for a year. On their range there was
an abundance of food and water, and during that
period I could always find them, their home being a
little hilly island in the prairie covered with timber
and brush, and detached from any irregular land by
several miles of grass.

Some authorities have placed woodcock shooting first in the list, and called it the fox-hunting of those pleasures in which the dog and gun form the chief accessories. As far as present British field-sports are concerned, I believe they are correct, but should the ruffed grouse be introduced, and they once experienced the suddenness of their rise, the velocity and irregularity of their flight, the uncertainty of their movements, and the beauty and size of this game when bagged, they would assuredly insert a saving clause, or change their opinions *in toto.* Much as I have said in favor of the American partridge, with equal fervor I can advance the claims of the ruffed grouse; still, they both are very different, but the nearest explanation I can at present think of, is that the former is essentially adapted to the requirement of the veteran sportsman, while the pursuit of the latter will tax all the strength of limb and impetuous ardor of our younger enthusiasts; the one is game that will afford the most delightful pastime, similar to hare-hunting with beagles, while the other will demand in its successful pursuit all the energy of the highly bred, dashing, courageous fox-hound. I doubt not many, I believe all, of the warm admirers of shooting, will agree with me, that there is a supe-

rior pleasure in making a mixed bag, now a mallard,
next a woodcock, perchance thirdly, a partridge, and
so forth—loading your discharged barrel, scarcely
knowing at what description of game it will be used.
Yes, truly, constant novelty and change is a great
additional attraction even in field sports, and with
our demesnes, parks, and forests, inhabited by a
goodly number of both these varieties, the ruffed
grouse and American partridge, in addition to their
present tenants, the cravings of the most insatiable
ought to be satisfied; and at a very trifling expense
and trouble these introductions could be accomplished.

GUN FOR GENERAL FOREIGN SHOOTING.

THERE is no gun so generally useful for all descriptions of shooting on the American Continent, in my humble opinion, as one of the following dimensions : viz., twenty-six inches long in the barrel, ten bore, and weighing about eight pounds. These dimensions are those of my constant and well-tried old companion, and I have never met with a gun that could perform better. A gun-maker in New York, who has deservedly a good reputation, told me that the best-shooting guns he had ever made were of these dimensions. If any intend ordering a gun for American shooting, I should further recommend that it be perfectly plain, and free from all engraving. As to choice between muzzle and breech loaders, I should advise the former, as cartridges are troublesome and bulky to carry, and if the stock should run short, a considerable loss of time would occur (if you were on the confines of civilization) before a fresh supply could be obtained, but there is no place, from a trading-post to a hamlet, where the ordinary loose ammunition can not be obtained.   Further, I am of opinion that the muzzle-loader has greater force, killing farther and hitting harder than the breech-loader.

CHINESE OYSTERS.

In my wanderings about the Chinese coast in search of game, I frequently came across immense banks of oysters, apparently no person's property; and this is the more remarkable when we remember that there is probably no people on the face of the globe who have the same skill in rendering all descriptions of animal matter fit for table purposes. About thirty miles from Victoria, the capital of Hong Kong, on the route to the entrance of the Canton River, is situated the entrance to a bay, which from the distance it runs inland is designated Deep Bay; the northern shore is one continuous mud-bank, on the upper portion of which are to be found actually acres of oysters. My acquaintance with this fact is not likely to be forgotten. A friend and I had been shooting wild fowl; a cripple had given us a long chase toward shore, and after we had succeeded in capturing the bird, we found our return cut off, as the tide had receded, and the

sharp edges of the oyster shells become so close to
the bottom of the boat, that if we had persevered
in forcing her out, we should soon have cut a hole
in her bottom. To get out and wade was impossible, as shoe leather would never have stood
the ordeal, therefore there was no alternative left
but to remain till the rising tide would float us out ;
any thing but a pleasant resource, when time was
valuable and shooting at a premium. Slightly to
console our wounded feelings, we attacked the
oysters, which were excellent, and certainly de-
molished an immense quantity. Another time, in
a pheasant-shooting trip to Meer's Bay, one of the
minor inlets, where our lorcha was anchored, had
its margin densely covered with oysters, and the
natives did not make the slightest objection to our
using as many as required. From this circumstance it may be presumed that they knew no
marketable value for them, for if a Chinaman can
have the slightest grounds for fabricating an excuse
for squeezing an Englishman, he is certain to do it.
The only oysters that I have known exposed for
sale in Hong Kong, and those only in very small
quantities, when they are always purchased by the
Europeans, are from Amoy, and they are really

excellent, for from appearance and flavor they can favorably compare with those of Colchester. For some years the resident merchants of Hong Kong have been aware of the fact, and like Shanghai mutton and game, the representatives of head-quarters at the port of Amoy annually send pro-pitiatory offerings of their delicate shell-fish to their superiors. Some time since I was informed that a considerable shipment of oysters was about to take place, with the intention of making an effort to furnish Australia and New Zealand with this luxury. Now instead of taking them from here, if the coast of China was selected, the probabilities of success in my opinion would be much greater, for the transportation distance can scarcely be over one-fourth of the voyage to Europe, and moreover, in favorable seasons any thing but a stormy passage might be anticipated, a circumstance not without considerable importance, for it is well known that the oyster can support itself a long time out of water on its own juice. If this hint should be adopted, then I have neither wasted the ink and paper with which this is indited, nor my time in giving my readers the information that oysters are to be obtained in the Celestial Empire.

CUTTLE-FISH.

THERE are very few inhabitants of the ocean which have so extensive a range of residence as the cuttle-fish. In the Atlantic or Pacific he is equally at home, and in the western end of the Mediterranean he abounds. Wondrous stories are told of his savage proclivities, and in a shop in China I saw a picture in which one of this family was represented embracing a junk (which, judging from the size of the figures on board, must have been two or three hundred tons), and quietly helping himself to mariners, as appetite dictated. Why the Celestials did not get under the hatches I was unable to comprehend. That some of this species grow to an immense size, there is no doubt, as the whale is often found to contain dismembered arms and other parts of this their favorite food, which must originally have been component parts of monsters of gigantic proportions. To their belligerent disposition I can attest, for well I remember seeing one about five feet across, attempting to seize a retriever who was paddling in the shallow water at the head of Rosia Bay, Gibraltar. During my residence in that garrison, there resided a señorita who, from her graceful carriage and pretty feet, never failed to attract attention; but she always wore her mantilla so disposed that her face could not be seen. Curiosity induced me to inquire the reason from one of her acquaintances, when I was informed that while bathing she had been seized by a cuttle-fish across the face, and that ever since an unsightly mark, where the blood had been drawn to the surface, remained. The cuttle-fish, although most repulsive to look at, is much prized on the coast of Spain as an article of food; they are frequently taken on the hook, but more generally caught among the rocks in shallow water with a gaff. A number of such in a boat doubtless would be considered unpleasant companions, for out of the water they can move with facility; however, this is not so, for the fisherman immediately on bringing him to the surface, with his hands turns the globe which forms the body inside out, thereby destroying all the power of suction. This is easily done, for there is an orifice on one side which the fingers can be forced into, and unless the fish should be of unusual size, no difficulty is experienced in placing him *hors de combat.* I have often eaten them; their flesh when properly cooked being excellent. The best mode of preparing them according to my taste, is the following : first cleanse thoroughly by scalding, then rub body and legs with garlic, afterward cut the whole into small pieces, which fry in olive oil, one or two fresh plucked Chili peppers being introduced for seasoning.

THE SNIPE OF AMERICA.

(SCOLOPAX WILSONII.)

I NEVER met a good shot who was not partial
to snipe shooting; whether I am a good shot or
no, matters not; but of all pleasures, there are few I
so thoroughly enjoy as a day among the long bills.
In the different portions of the globe that fate
or luck has knocked me about, I have always been
able to find snipe; so I am inclined to believe that
there is no family more generally and universally
distributed. But the prairies of Western America
far outdo all others in the abundance of this description of feathered game. *Scolopax Wilsonii* is truly
a splendid bird, so nearly similar to our own home
beauty that the skillful naturalist is alone able to
distinguish the one from the other; in habits, flight,
and even call, they are essentially alike. How my
heart warmed the first day I shot them, for the
familiar cry that each bird uttered as he flushed,

transported me back to days long gone by, to the society of old companions long under the sod, and a happy circle of relations, to whom it was ever my delight to exhibit the proofs of my skill.

The Wilson snipe—for by this name he is familiarly known all over the American continent—spends the winter months in the Southern States, principally in those that border the Gulf of Mexico; but as spring advances, they follow up northward the line of demarkation between frost and thaw, ultimately arriving in that boundless expanse which stretches northward from the Great Lakes to the Arctic Ocean. Up in this remote haunt is their principal breeding-ground, although occasionally a nest may be found much farther to the south; but in all instances of such that I have been able to find, I have been induced to believe that either the male or female bird had met with an accident, preventing the following of the migration of his or her companions. What a beautiful lesson all may learn from this; how it should speak home to the human heart this attachment of the mate, who, sooner than desert a companion, forsakes for the time being his whole race, save one, and foregoes even following the journey dictated by nature.

In southern Illinois, where I had the greatest amount of experience in killing this game, the advance heralds of migration generally arrived about the 10th of March. Much, of course, depended whether the winter was late or otherwise; but if a thaw had taken place, and a moist southerly wind had been blowing over night, the ground that yesterday you had tramped over in pursuit of wild duck without seeing a single snipe, on the morrow would harbor thousands. Their journey being a continuation of short flights, they are seldom out of condition on arrival; and as they do not take up a permanent residence, little compunction is felt in shooting them. Out of the large number that I have brought to bag, I do not remember a single instance of an egg, or other indication that pairing had taken place. The prairies of this State (Illinois) are generally burned late in the fall, or early in spring, to improve the succeeding year's grazing, leaving the surface of the soil entirely denuded of grass, except where moisture has prevented the burn taking effect. Over this, especially in the vicinity of sloughs, dwarf persimmon bushes abound, and there the snipe much frequent. A dog is not necessary here, for the game is so abundant, unless, perhaps, a good retriever, who must be under such control as never to attempt to leave heel, except when ordered by his master to recover a cripple. A further attraction to this sport, beyond the numbers that can be killed, is that few days pass on which numbers of teal, pin-tailed duck, or mallard do not assist to swell the size of your game-bag. From the advent of the first flight till the middle of May, additional arrivals take place, but after that date all disappear till the fall of the leaf, and gusty changeable weather fortells the near approach of winter. But the autumnal flight is never numerically equal to that of spring; still, if twenty brace will satisfy the sportsman, he can have that reward for his labor, provided he be a fair shot.

In America are to be found many excellent shots. By them the arrival of the snipe is looked forward to with much pleasure; but to the pot-hunter, the fellow who will shoot pinnated grouse on the ground, the duck upon the water, or crawl all day through brush to have a standing chance at a wild turkey, this branch of shooting presents little attraction. How satisfactory it is that there is at least one game-bird who can laugh with derision at such pursuers. At first, when the snipe makes its appearance, especially if the weather be wet and blustering, they are inclined to be wild; but much depends upon the amount of cover, and consequently shelter, afforded by the locality, but when the genial sun of spring shines with invigorating warmth, they will frequently lie so close that many will flush almost at your feet. When wild, their flights are long and rapid; when not so, they droop their wings, and frequently alight before a hundred yards have been traversed. However, this does not apply to the whole day, for toward sunset, possibly from having by that time digested their last night's meal, for they feed principally by night, they invariably become wild, and more difficult of access. To be successful in making a heavy bag of snipe, there is a rule which may be beneficial to the tyro to remember, viz., always to hunt down wind, or as much so as possible, provided always dogs are not used. The stronger the breeze, the more necessity for doing so; the reason being, that invariably snipe fly against the wind, and being flushed by your advancing on them from windward, the birds will wheel round to the right or left, and present an easy cross-shot, in their determination to pursue the desired direction.

The migration of this snipe, as well as of the American woodcock, is peculiar; all appear to act independently of the other. Dozens may be seen to pass or light near you in the space of a few minutes, yet each bird is alone. Many an evening, after sunset, have I watched their coming, yet never saw two or more together. As a rule, these journeys by both the above-mentioned take place before sunrise and after sunset. This scattered mode of traveling, and the hour at which it takes place, are doubtless the reasons that none but close observers of nature witness these flights. By the end of May the migration of this snipe has ceased, and their summer quarters are reached, which are, as previously stated, principally north of the Great Lakes and the St. Lawrence; although not a few spend the summer in Nova Scotia, New Brunswick, and Maine. Early in June they commence laying their eggs, four in number, in a nest of the most primitive construction, it being simply an indentation in some trifling excrescence of the surface. The eggs, which are of a yellowish-brown color, blotched with dark markings, taper very much toward the small end; they are always placed in the nest with the larger end outward. As soon as the young are hatched, they leave the nest, and in six weeks afterward are almost full grown. At this age it is impossible to tell the Wilson snipe from our home variety; however, at any period the difference is very slight; and as they are quite as strong, swift, and erratic in their flight, and, moreover, to be found in immense quantities, ten or twelve dozen per day being no unusual bag in March, those who can spare time and money would, if fond of this description of shooting, find ample recompense by a visit across the Atlantic.

A BIG BUCK.

In the autumn of 186-, when traveling across the Grand Prairie, I got caught in the first snow-storm of the season. The vicinity was but sparsely settled, and from the thickness of the drift our charioteer lost his way, and after getting mired times without number, and enduring one of the most disagreeable nights out of doors it is possible to imagine, we reached the village of Kent. Under ordinary circumstances it would have presented no great inducements, but the large wood fire that blazed in the bar-room of the diminutive tavern, after our protracted night of hardship, possessed such attractions, that I determined to lie over for a couple of days. The neighborhood was well stocked with game I learned the following evening, when I presented myself among the *habitués*, who commonly made this public-house their place of rendezvous after the toils of the day. No small portion of the conversation was in reference to a buck, who for years had constantly been seen, yet none of the heretofore successful hunters had been able to circumvent him. It was evident that this animal was of no ordinary size, as he was dubbed by all with the *sobriquet* of the big buck, and one regular old leather-stocking, whose opinion was always listened to with the reverence due to an authority, ventured to assert that he believed the bullet would never be molded that would tumble him (the buck) in his tracks. This extraordinary deer had almost escaped my memory, and I was resting over my next morning's pipe, and beginning to fear that my visit was longer than necessary, for there was absolutely nothing to do but eat and sleep, unless the prices of pork, corn, or wheat had possessed an interest; when a man from the timber land arrived with a load of wood, and held the following conversation with the mixer of mint-juleps, cocktails, etc. "Abe, have you e'er a shooting-iron that you can loan this coon?"

Abe having replied in the negative, and inquired the reason, was told that the most alfiestest big buck had crossed the road about a mile off, and gone into the Squire's corn.* Quietly going to my

* Every person in Western America is either Squire or Colonel.

bedroom, I unpacked my heaviest gun, a ten bore, in whom I have particular faith, and having noted the route that the teamster had come by, I followed the back track of his sled, and true enough found the prints of a very heavy buck. The day was still young, myself in good walking-trim, and with an internal determination not to be beaten, except night overtook me, and very probably with the hope to show the neighbors that a Britisher was good for some purposes, I followed the track with unusually willing steps and light heart. To get into the corn-field the buck had jumped the snake fence and afterward doubled back, and as the wind did not suit for me to enter at the same place, I made a considerable *détour*. In my right barrel I had sixteen buck-shot, about the size that would run one hundred to the pound, and a bullet in the left. As the corn had not yet been gathered, and the undergrowth of cuckle-burs and other weeds was tolerably dense; I had little doubt but that I would get sufficiently close to make use of the former. An old stager like my quarry, I knew from experience would be desperately sharp, so with the utmost caution I advanced up wind, eyes and ears strained to the utmost tension. I had only got about a fourth of the field traversed, when I heard some voices right to windward encouraging a dog to hold a pig. The noise of the men, dog, and porker, I concluded would start the game off in the reverse direction, so hurriedly retracing my steps, I regained the fence, got over it, and took my stand at an angle that stretched close to a slough which was densely covered with a growth of various aquatic weeds and rushes. In about five minutes after gaining my position, I was greeted by a sight of the beauty, who hopped the fence where there was a broken rail, and gaining the opening, for a moment halted, then tossing up his head, offered me a fair cross-shot nearly eighty yards distant. Pitching my gun well in front, I pulled the trigger, and well I knew not fruitlessly, for he gave a short protracted jump, dropped his white tail close into his hams, and with an increased pace disappeared in the swamp.

Unless the wound was mortal, or so severe as to seriously incommode him, I was certain he would not be satisfied to remain in such close propinquity to danger, so after reloading I made a *détour* to find where he had left this cover to seek one more retired. My conjecture was correct, for after travel-

ing nearly half-a-mile, I found the familiar tell-
tale track. The snow was in pretty good order,
both for tracking and walking, and I did not let the
grass grow under my feet. As yet I had seen no
signs of blood, which the more thoroughly impressed
me that my lead had made more than a skin wound.
In about an hour's walking, I found myself on the
edge of another slough, which I was hesitating
whether to enter or go round, when I espied my
friend, some way beyond range, going over a neighboring swell of the prairie. Of course I cut off
the angle and cast forward to where the view was
obtained, and as I rose the swell, in the distance
I saw my friend at a stand-still, evidently anxiously
scrutinizing my direction. My cap was of a very
light color, so I concluded he did not see me, and
my supposition was again correct, for after a few
minutes he relaxed his pace, and turning at right
angles, walked into a small expanse of dense rushes,
interspersed with an occasional stunted willow. In
deer shooting, if you suppose an animal severely
wounded, never hurry him; if he once lie down,
and you give him time to stiffen, you will not have
half the trouble in his ultimate capture that you
would have by constantly keeping him on the

move. So I practiced in this instance; carefully for ten or fifteen minutes I watched that he did not leave the cover; then having concluded that he had lain down, I quietly lit my pipe and dawdled away an hour more. Deeming that I had granted sufficient law, I renewed operations and pushed forward; the track was very irregular in length of pace from where he had reduced his gait to a walk, and several times from want of lifting his feet high enough, he had scuffed the surface of the snow with his toes. An old deer-stalker will know these symptoms, a young one may without harm remember them. Having cautiously followed the trail three parts of the way across the cover, and almost commenced to think I would have done better by waiting half-an-hour longer, the buck jumped up within twenty yards, heading straight from me, when I gave him the contents a second time of the right-hand barrel in the back of his head.

The distance was too great to remove him home that day, so cutting a branch off a willow, I affixed my handkerchief to it, and left this banner waving to denote possession, also to furnish a hint to the prairie wolves that they had better steer clear. That night at the tavern bar in the most ostentatious manner, in presence of the assembled crowd, I ordered a team to be got ready in the morning to bring in the big buck; old leather-stocking, *sotto voce*, remarking, that I had not been reared on the right soil to be able to come that game. However, next morning, when I arrived with my trophy, the crowd congratulated me, while leather-stocking remarked, that he knew not what the world was coming to, by G—d, when a Britisher with a bird gun could kill the biggest buck in Illinois. In conclusion I would say, that in skinning we found that at the first shot one grain had gone through the lungs, while two more had lodged farther back. The gross weight of this deer was one hundred and eighty-four pounds.

BLACK BASS.

In advocating the introduction of birds, I ,feel I have not yet performed my work; bear with me further, and grant me space to advocate another introduction that, in my opinion, deserves the favorable attention of all lovers of the gentle art. Although I love the dog and gun, still I am equally devoted to the rod. As every season has its beauties and its fascinations, so has every variety of field sports. On a glorious September day, what can exceed the pleasure of following a brace of well-trained, well-bred, high-couraged dogs over the golden stubbles? On a mild spring day, with a soft southwest breeze and dark clouds overhead, can any thing be more delightful than following the tortuous course of a trout brook, taking from pool or stream the speckled beauties, or knee-deep in a rapid, boisterous river, first rising, now hooking, and perchance killing the glorious salmon? The whirr of pheasant or partridge is pleasant music; the voice of hounds

is not less so; but the screech of your reel, when
first you are fast to a heavy game-fish, is a song that
even Patti herself can not rival. For a fish to be
popular among fishermen, he must have three requisites, viz., gameness when hooked, boldness in feeding, and, when he has yielded his life, be a fit feast
for an epicure. All these requisites I claim for the
black bass; and, therefore, presume to lay his claims
for introduction before your numerous readers.
There is no section of the world so intersected by
rivers and lakes as the North American continent,
and in nearly all these waters, from northern Canada
to the tributaries of the Mississippi, and the various
waters that flow into the Gulf of Mexico, the black
bass is to be found. It matters not whether it be
river or lake; whether the water be clear or muddy,
stagnant or rapid; in all he appears equally to
flourish. What splendid homes could we offer him
here! All our ornamental waters, though generally
unsuited to trout, would be retreats eminently fitted
to his nature; and the fishermen, instead of capturing such common pluckless fish as bream, tench,
carp, or even perch, would have an antagonist that
would test all his skill, the stoutness and endurance
of his tackle, with that untiring, unflinching resolu-
5

tion and headstrong energy which no other fresh-water fish of the same size, I believe, possesses.

The black bass is an extremely free feeder, and is caught in all the various ways used to capture trout. He rises freely at the fly; with minnow or worm, craw-fish, spoon bait, or almost any artificial device, he can be taken. On being hooked, generally the first effort he makes for freedom is to spring from the water. Look out, Mr. Angler, dip your rod in courtesy to him, for if you neglect the requisite *salam*, your acquaintance will probably terminate. When this device has failed, with a purpose and force alike surprising, he makes a rush for parts unknown, and not until every effort, every trick is put in practice, that is known to the fish family, can you get the slightest chance to use your landing net. I have frequently, after a long and fierce struggle, been about to place the net under him, but the movement was enough; though apparently exhausted, the fish took a new lease of life, and a further trial of patience was demanded before I could call the prize mine. In shape, the black bass much resembles a well-fed trout; but is deeper and thicker made, while the tail is remarkable for its breadth. Their weight varies from one pound to five pounds;

yet on the Niagara River, near the village of Chippewa, I captured a splendid fellow, quite eight pounds;
but I was then assured that I had reason to con-
gratulate myself, for fish of such a size were far from
common. The color, as in all varieties of fish, varies
much. In clear running water they are generally a
very dark green upon the back (much such a shade
as the darker hues in mackerel), gradually getting
lighter, almost to white, as you approach the abdo-
men; but in those Southern waters, which are
strongly impregnated with alluvial deposit, and consequently turbid, the back of these bass is less
brilliant in shade, while the stomach is not so clear a
white. A still further advantage that may recommend them is, that they are in season when trout
should not be killed. In spring they spawn, the
exact time varying in different waters on account of
season and position as to latitude.

If I may judge from the quantity of spawn the
female contains, they must be immensely prolific;
for although the individual ovum is small, the roe is
very large in proportion to the bulk of the fish.
From my own observation and inquiries, I believe
that the spawn is from sixteen to twenty days in
maturing, after being deposited, which would give

ample time for its transportation across the Atlantic.
I am further of opinion that, indiscriminately, gravel
or soil bottom is selected on which to deposit the
eggs; for many of the rivers and ponds in which I
have captured this bass flowed through, or were
situated in deep bottom-lands, where a stone, even
as large as a pebble, would be difficult to find.   One
pond in southern Illinois I particularly remember;
it covered a space of about thirty acres, with an
average depth of about three feet, except in the
southern extremity, where about eight feet of water
could be found.   The bottom was entirely composed
of mud; yet this pond swarmed with black bass.
Lake Champlain, the St. Lawrence, and Lake
Ontario (all who have visited these regions will
remember) are remarkably clear, with gravelly or
rocky bottoms, and each is a favorite haunt of this
fish.   I mention this to prove the better how universal a favorite and extensive his adoption might
become.

A friend, once a resident of the Isle of Skye, and
a well-known successful trout and salmon fisherman,
had a beautiful little lake, about ten acres in extent,
on his estate, not many miles from Toronto, which
he had stocked with black bass.   In a few years

their numbers so much increased, that in an hour or two, trolling of an evening, a dozen or more could easily be taken. This lake had neither outlet or inlet, but was supplied with water from springs in the bottom.

I fear it will be almost deemed heresy to place this fish on a par with the trout; at least, some such idea I had when I first heard the two compared; but I am bold, and will go farther. I consider he is the superior of the two, for he is equally good as an article of food, and much stronger and untiring in his efforts to escape when hooked.

By all means let us have black bass introduced. I feel confident this fish requires but to be known to be most highly appreciated.

HINTS TO YOUNG ANGLERS.

I can not hope to teach the expert, but I doubt not that there are many of the younger readers of this little work who may be assisted in taking a larger basket of fish than they otherwise would, by a knowledge of the following artifices, which I have often found most successful. In a clear, warm day, at the termination of the green drake season, when the trout can not be induced to rise at the artificial fly, I have frequently been most successful by practicing the following *ruse*, viz., having only a trail fly on your casting-line (which should be very long and light), make it slightly fast to a water-lily or other leaf; having marked where a fish is feeding, go up stream well above the place, and guide, through means of your rod, the leaf, so that it will pass close by the spot, taking the precaution of using a long line, and to keep as much out of sight as possible; when the leaf has reached the trout's haunt, by a slight strike disengage your fly from the leaf, so that it will drop in the water, and but seldom will the fish hesitate to rise, and on such occasions will yourself fail to strike successfully. Now for hint number two: when I have been unable to get a strike minnow fishing, I have stimulated the trout's appetite, by taking a worm and hooking it transversely across the center, so that when your minnow is put on, both sides of the worm hang on either side of his head. If fish reason, I suppose they thus argue: That fellow is going off with a prize; if he was not in good health, he would scarcely have such a voracious appetite. It's evident Mister Fisherman has played no tricks on this chap. So at him he goes, and tyro's basket becomes heavier by another fish. Not to keenness but to accident I made this discovery. I had fished most unsuccessfully for several hours, having changed from worm to minnow and *vice versâ* ; in one of these alterations, being careless from want of success, some worm was left on the shank of the hook after I reverted to the minnow: the hint was not lost, and often afterward practiced.

THE AMERICAN THOROUGH-BRED.

I THINK that few will disagree with me that horse-racing was established not alone for the amusement it affords, but for the encouragement of breeding a superior stamp of animal, alike capable of speed and endurance. Of late years the former quality has been the desideratum, and to so great a pitch has it come through light weights, short races, &c., that the most useless, as far as utility purposes may be considered, are patronized for sires. The result is, what would have been deemed a race-horse a quarter of a century ago, is now thought a hunter at best, while what our fathers would have condemned as a weedy tucked-up brute, we, with our advanced views of civilization, call a race-horse. Speed for a short distance is what all harp after, and if stamina with speed can not be obtained, the more useful quality is neglected, or entirely sacrificed, for a second less time in a mile race. Double the length of the race—make the course two miles instead of one—and which would be first at the winning-post?—or, still better, make the race three miles, and I much doubt if the weed would come home at all, leave alone save his distance.

Much injury is doubtless done our horses by running them long before they reach maturity. If you take a growing boy and over-tax his strength, what will be the result? A wreck before he reaches manhood. So it is with our thorough-bred colts and fillies. They are forced forward like hot-house plants, prematurely reach maturity of form, when they are put to work trying even to aged animals, their muscular development being still soft and unset, and consequently unequal to the task, causing a broken-down cripple at the very time when, if permitted to have followed Nature's dictates, the poor creature would have rejoiced in all the perfections of beauty that charm the eye and tell of speed and endurance. What an every-day occurrence it is to hear of such and such a colt, immense favorites with the public from their success as two-year olds, being scratched? And why? In some closely-contested struggle, when flesh and blood was doing its utmost, under whip and spur,

5*

a yet further exertion was called for, and from the
effort a strain or injury was received which time
ultimately developed; and thus the flower of the
stable, the hope of the owner, is thrown out of
work, ultimately to descend through the gradations
from pampered pet to over-wrought cab-horse.
True, it is not unfrequently the lot of man to
undergo the same vicissitudes of fortune; but he
invariably has some hand in altering his position.
But the poor horse earns degradation through his
endeavor to serve a selfish master too well.

The Americans are justly considered close observers and an essentially practical people, possessed
with that energy which has long characterized this
their mother people. From being originally thrown
in a new land, where every effort and resource had
to be employed to raise them to the standard of
older countries, constant required attention to all
the details of life, through numerous generations,
has made them what they are, inferior to none, and
far, far ahead of many European powers who can
date their existence back numerous centuries. At
an early age the inherent love of Englishmen for
horse-racing showed itself in America; and as might
be expected, when the importation of thorough-bred

stock took place, such judgment was employed, that
the best animals that could be obtained in England
were only introduced. Unfortunately, however,
racing got into bad repute, from the number of
mauvais sujets it attracted, and although the
Southern gentlemen did their utmost to cleanse
away the stain, the fanatical puritanical spirit of
many Northern States, tabooed the institution for
years; thus it only had a partial existence, and
but few horses were imported, and those always
to the South; but if the number was small, the
selections were the more carefully made. However,
again a revival took place, principally at first
through the instrumentality of the late Mr. Atchison Alexander, of Woodford, Kentucky, and latterly
through the efforts of Mr. Jerome, of New York;
so that at the present date almost every State
boasts one or two race-courses, where as fine racing
can be enjoyed as at home. From an innate love
of the horse, I not only visited the majority of the
American races, but obtained the *entrée* to many
of the training and breeding establishments; thus
gaining opportunities of forming opinions, that
defective judgment alone would cause to be incorrect. One only of these establishments will I

mention, because I was more conversant with it, not because it was either the largest or most replete with conveniences,—that of Mr. Sanford, in New Jersey, about thirty miles from the metropolis. This gentleman had a large number of all ages at work, all his own, for he was not a public trainer, but a person of affluence, loving the horse for his beauty and use, and running them with the hope that if they were entitled to the laurels they would bear them. In close proximity to his stables was his private training-ground, and the buildings were replete with every convenience that ingenuity, art, or money could supply. In looking over his pets, numerous descendants of *imp.* Hedgeford, Glencoe, Knight of St. George, &c., were found, all good ones, as some old memories will recall, and closely allied to the American-bred cracks, Lexington, Boston, Kentucky, and Asteroid. One thing that can not fail to strike the English visitors, is the much greater amount of stamina that all appear to possess over our home-bred animal; and I am inclined to believe that this is not only show. I am aware that an English nobleman, probably the most successful of modern times on the turf, thought the same, and in consequence introduced a stallion. However, the importation did not turn out a success; but might he not have been injured in the voyage, or the purchaser been wrong in his selection? To successfully clear a rasper, there is nothing like going boldly at it; so, without further preamble, I believe that the introduction of a good American stallion would be beneficial to those who want to breed weight-carrying, fast, lasting horses.

Three or four miles is no unfrequent distance for a race to be run across the Atlantic, and it has always struck me how wonderfully game all appeared to finish, something like the Irishman's car-horse, a spurt always remaining to take your honor to the hall-door.

The Americans run their youngsters in their two-year-old form, but the weights up are very light, the distances short, and the ordeal seldom required oftener than three or four times in a season; therefore the occasion of accident that our colts of the same age suffer from is materially reduced; in fact, if scratching in the United States was as frequent as here, where the number of entries does not exceed one-fourth of ours, they would have few or no horses show at the post.

For three and four year olds, the old system of

heats is much in vogue; no bad one, let me say,
for proving endurance; and here again I was much
pleased with the gameness with which the con-
testants always re-assembled. At Seacaucus, near
New York, there is a bi-annual meeting; the establishment is superintended by a most hospitable,
kind-hearted old Virginian, whose heart is in his
work. I attended one of the meetings here, in
which a son of Knight of St. George won a heat
race; it was so closely contested, and so gamely
finished, that it even now warms my blood while I
write of it. The winner was a dark bay, wonderfully compact in build, with a few gray hairs at the
setting on of the tail, so common a mark of many
of his family. What a charger, I thought to myself, he would make; nor do I believe. I was
far wrong. That day this horse proved himself a
good one at long distances, and in heats, but he has
also made his mile in one minute and forty-six
seconds—reliable time. Now, this horse, Knight-
hood by name, if I remember correctly, had not
been galloped off his feet when a two-year old, or
he never could have undergone successfully the
trial he endured on the occasion mentioned. At
Paterson, New Jersey, I witnessed another closely

contested heat race; the winner was a mare of Mr.
Sanford's, called Nanny Butler; she was an un-
commonly well-put-together undersized nag, but
with the most unsightly height of withers; five
heats had to be run before the race was decided.
The mare was ridden by a well-known veteran
jockey, black as my hat; his reputation was great,
and that day proved not without reason; still a
good jockey can't land a bad mount first, although
a good jockey can materially assist a good horse.
At the start, the odds were heavy against her, and
when she was declared winner, not the mare, but
the rider, got the credit from the shrewd public.
Why not have divided the praise? But such is too
frequently the way of the world. Now, if Nanny
had been run to death—or I will say had done the
work of Achievement in her two-year old form—is
it reasonable to suppose that she would have gamely
and uninjured finished as winner the last and fifth
heat of a two-mile-heat race?

I was in New York when the beautiful Jerome
Park race-course was to be opened. Kentucky was
then the acknowledged crack of Eastern stables,
but away south of the Ohio River was his half-
brother, both being sons of the famous Lexington.

Wonderful rumors had reached the Atlantic sea-board of what the Western representative could do. For a long time it was doubtful whether this great gun would put in an appearance. So Kentucky was backed at immense odds for the great event—the Inauguration Stakes. At length a telegraph arrived, announcing the intention of Mr. Alexander to forward his horse Asteroid. Public opinion became divided, but, as is generally the case, drifted back to the home favorite. Asteroid arrived a few days before the meeting, but unfortunately broke down; however, I availed myself of an opportunity to inspect him, and such a horse I have seldom looked at—a hunter up to fourteen stone across any country —yet there was not a single gross point about him. To what his mishap could be attributed, few could say; but I learned that, for an American horse, he had done an unusual amount of work in his younger days.

Kentucky, the most successful, and possibly the best horse that has been produced in America in modern days, although differing in color, is very much like Blair Athole in form, very showy and cocky in his action, and of most desirable temper. He has, I believe, only once been beaten, and then by Norfolk, a half-brother, who was shortly afterward transported to the Pacific slope; however, this defeat was to be attributed to (as I have been informed by a most reliable person) being out of condition. He is also a son of Lexington, and therefore claims relationship to Boston and *Imp.* Glencoe, ancestors to whom he truly does no discredit. I have seen Kentucky run several times, but always was he so immensely superior to his antagonists, that the race was quite one-sided. At Saratoga, I believe, on one occasion, his jockey pricked him, but I much doubt if such was necessary.

Lexington I have frequently mentioned; I much regret that I forget his genealogical tree. As a sire and race-horse, his superior in the Western hemisphere was never produced. One performance was his running at the Great State Race on Metaire course, New Orleans, a four-mile-heat race, in which one of the heats was made in 7 minutes 19¾ seconds—a performance his owner might well be proud of—for I can find no record of its being excelled; and it must be remembered that American time is always correctly taken by reliable persons, and published at the end of each heat or race. Lexington still lives, and is the sire of numerous progeny, many of whom I know, and all except one who shall be nameless, are not only fast, but enduring horses.

In conclusion, whether the American thorough-bred is as fast as ours would be difficult to decide; but that he is a most lasting, enduring, game horse, I can assert, a proof that the Americans have not forgotten, in the universal mania of the age for fastness, the desideratum endurance—the *sine quâ non* for utility.

HOW TO CAPTURE GRAY MULLET.

OFTEN I have stood on the fluvial portion of a river and watched the gray mullet freely sporting on the surface. Numerous were the efforts I made to catch these wily gentry with hook and line; but all overtures were rejected, and the fish preferred declining the bait to leaving their element. The gray mullet feeds principally on the surface, more particularly in warm weather, and as they are remarkably shy and gifted with but small mouths, with a preference to sucking in the bait, to freely swallowing like trout or others, the difficulties in the way of capturing them are obvious, and hence I will explain a method some might call poaching, but really no more so than trimmer fishing; in truth, it is much more excusable, for by the latter you capture fish that freely take the hook, while on the other hand you ensnare rogues that all your skill and patience will fail otherwise to bring to bag. Obtain a piece of flat cork about one inch in depth and the size of a regular ship biscuit; have a pouch made of coarse gauze, in which a slice of bread, the size of the cork can be placed, the gauze retaining the bread flat against the cork. From the margin of the cork suspend around the bread a dozen hooks, about the size of those usually employed in trout bait fishing, these hooks to be tied on strong gut, six inches long, and on the points of a few of them a small dice of bread should be placed. Armed with half a dozen of these infernal machines, and provided with a landing net, go in your boat above where the mullet are known to resort, drop your corks in the water, about eight or ten yards apart, scattering some crumbs among them, and let the tide or current float them to the fish, keeping the boat a good way in the rear. Don't be in a hurry, the fish will not keep you long waiting; each float will soon be surrounded, and when the mullet find that they can not carry away the bread wholesale, they will knock the floats with their noses, slap them with their tails, and in a few seconds you will have a prize on each trimmer, hooked by back, tail, or side. If the captives run large much sport will be enjoyed in retaking your floats, for it is wonderful how long a four or five

pound fish will manage to avoid you.   This method
I have practiced often, both in smooth and rough
water, and never without meeting with the greatest
success, not only with the gray mullet but many
other species.

THE PINNATED GROUSE.

(TETRAO CUPIDO.)

THE first pheasant I killed in China I thought the noblest game-bird that ever I had pulled a trigger upon, and truly he was a beauty; the plumage was in the most perfect state—the neck of the greenest emerald, the ring of the purest white, the tail the longest, and the different shades and tints of wings and body the very brightest I had ever seen in one of his species; moreover, he weighed nearly one-half more than any of the same family I had killed at home, and to add additional appreciation, the shot that brought him to the ground was a difficult one and at long range. For years the pheasant of the southern portion of China reigned paramount in my opinion; but a change has come over my ideas, and now superlative before all others, I place two varieties of American game-birds. What days of pleasure have I had in the pursuit of pinnated grouse; what splendid bags have I made, and on such ground

as gave my darling companion setters the very best
opportunities of showing their sagacity and careful
education to the greatest advantage. In my previous notice of the ruffed grouse (*Tetrao umbellus*), I
have stated that I do not believe this bird (the pinnated grouse) so worthy of acclimatization as the
last mentioned; and why? he disregards distance
in his late autumnal flights; and therefore where
shooting ranges are limited by bounds, unless the
proprietors on every side would mutually agree for
their introduction and protection, I fear that the
labors of one landowner in introducing and propa-
gating them would be fraught with dissatisfaction,
as his neighbors would enjoy almost as much as
himself the benefit of his expense and trouble. But
for all that, the pinnated grouse is most worthy of
our attention; he is truly a most noble bird, and
affords the sportsman the best of sport, till the
cold winds preceding winter cause him to pack, in
the same manner as our red and black game, when
their wariness becomes so great that naught but
quick shooting and Ely's green cartridges are likely
to help the laborer to produce a bag remunerative
for his toil. That this bird could be acclimated here
there is no doubt, for he is capable of withstanding

great changes of temperature; is not particular as to choice of ground as long as it is open; and plenty of grain and grass seed can be obtained. Although his range is now principally confined to the prairie country of the United States, not being found in great numbers till the edge of the Grand Prairie is reached, still formerly he was found equally abundant all over the open lands; still, however, Long Island and the island of Martha's Vineyard possess some remnants, who long since would have disappeared but for the protection and care of the landowners in those places, who have endeavored to prevent if possible the extinction of this valuable bird upon their estates. I can not well imagine any place so bleak in winter as the scrub uplands of the two aforementioned islands, unless, perhaps, Mull and Jura on the Scotch coast. The bird that could with impunity withstand the rigors of the cold in the former could doubtless with impunity do the same in the latter. The pinnated grouse pairs in March, and generally produces from twelve to fourteen young at a brood; the chicks very early take to the wing, but their flight is weak and short until they are more than half grown. During the infancy of the family, the courage and artifice of the parent

bird to intimidate or draw off intruders is worthy of
notice. At first she will fly toward you as if intent
on doing you battle, but when this course has failed,
she will retire, droop her wings, struggle on the
ground, only just keeping beyond your grasp, always
moving in a direction contrary to where her brood
are hid, until parent instinct tells her that the children are safe, when suddenly on strong wings she
will start for a distant flight. The facility with
which the young secrete themselves is most surprising. Frequently have I got unexpectedly into the
center of a family, when up they would rise like a
flight of bees and as rapidly drop again; certainly
you see the exact spot on which they have alighted
—that tuft of grass you believe most surely contains one, but search as you will, turn over carefully every blade, look well about the roots—all is
useless, for no fledgeling will you find.

At the commencement of the pairing season, particularly if the weather is calm and cloudy, the male
birds will be heard calling all day; their note resembling the lowing of a cow, which can be heard
distinctly for over a mile. At this time fierce-look-
ing encounters appear to take place, but I am inclined
to believe that their fights are all a sham, performed

6

to show themselves to the greatest advantage before
the admiring ladies who assemble around; for I have
never been able to find a maimed hero, and seldom
more than a broken feather resulting from the con-
test.   As the spring advances they restrict their calling to evening and morning, and by the time the
brood is hatched, cease it altogether. The peculiarity of the call of the males of this species is such,
that once heard, it is difficult to forget, particularly
when softened by distance; it is produceed by forcing the air out of two orange-colored receptacles
placed on either side of the throat, and which, when
inflated, are as large in circumference as a man's fin-
ger, perfectly free from feathers upon their surface,
but hid when in a state of quiescence by fan-shaped
bunches of hackles that completely cover them.*

   The pinnated grouse is about the size of our pheasant; however, they differ considerably, those birds
that inhabit southern Illinois being at least one-fourth
larger than those obtained in Minnesota, Wisconsin,
and the northwest prairies. They are of a beautiful
mottled brown and fawn color, frequently with white
finger-marks on the upper portion of the wings and

---

* The most killing hackles for tying trout-flies.

back, are feathered down the legs to the feet, have beautifully set-on small heads, with a slight crest, and bright yellow iris. When standing, their attitude is very erect, but graceful, while their flight is strong and swift, more especially late in the season. On being flushed, they invariably cackle, and the first flight, except of young birds, is always long. In the commencement of the season, and in fact as long as the weather is bright and mild, they lie remarkably well to dogs; but as soon as severe and cold weather sets in, they pack and become wild. However, late in October, if you should hit upon a warm, summer-like day, the birds will lie so remarkably close between the hours of 10 A. M. and 3 P. M., that marvelous bags can be made.

As a delicacy, this bird can favorably compare with any of the grouse family, but is dissimilar in one respect from all the others, for the sooner it is cooked after being killed, the more delicate and savory it will be found. Even the skill of Delmonico, in New York, the justly celebrated restaurant proprietor, with all his knowledge of *cuisine*, can not impart the flavor that the same bird would have had from the hands of the most ignorant cook, provided it was served a few hours after it was killed.

The pinnated grouse can easily be domesticated. Mr. Audubon, the naturalist, for some time kept quite a number in a walled garden, where they became as tame as domestic fowls; nor do I believe there would be any difficulty in transporting them across the Atlantic. To gentlemen stocking preserves, or desirous of being able to show a great variety of game upon their estate, I believe this magnificent member of the grouse genus well worthy of attention.

FISHING AT GIBRALTAR.

DEAR old Gibraltar, much as thou art frequently railed at, I believe the faults are more imaginary than real. Englishmen are grumblers proverbially and truly, more particularly the untraveled specimens. Transport them once away from native soil, and nothing that they see or make use of is equal to what is to be had at home. I am almost inclined to believe that there is a spirit of discontent in the breed, for our cousins across the Atlantic, although to a less degree, are strongly pregnated with the same peculiarity. Why is it that you seldom find one who is doing garrison duty at Gibraltar who does not sigh for change; true! you, if a subaltern, have more guards to keep, and in the cool season an overplus of brigade days, still you have your hounds, who, although they do not kill whenever they meet, afford plenty of fun; you have numerous pretty rides open to you into Spain, and if a fisherman or shot, sport can both be obtained in the bay and over the straits in the vicinity of Tangiers quite as good as you probably enjoyed at home, unless you had the privilege of a well-stocked salmon river or carefully preserved demesne. Although I am certain this garrison is seldom without numerous followers of old Izaak Walton, yet I dare bet that few have essayed their art while there—why, I can not say—for although I did constantly, I never met a companion, and more the pity; for fishing (that is, sea-fishing) is here to be obtained of the greatest excellence.

The New Mole, where vessels obtain their requisite fuel, used to be a favorite haunt of mine, more particularly on those serene, romantic nights peculiar to the Mediterranean, when with my light fly-rod and a small brilliant artificial minnow attached to very light tackle, I used to capture dozens of a beautiful little fish, of the mackerel family, there called horse-mackerel; true they were not large, seldom exceeding nine or ten inches in length, but then they were so game, giving as much sport as a half-pound trout, before you could safely land them on terra firma; and when fishing for these resplendent little beauties, you would occasionally hook a monster, when your only option was to give him the butt, place a check on your line, and force the weak portion of your tackle to

part. So often did this occur to me, that I determined
to go armed for emergencies; and having obtained
a most powerful bamboo-rod and attached a salmon reel, with a sardine for bait, I determined to try
the results, nor was I long kept in suspense; the rush
came, line was given, but all of no avail, for the hoped-
for captive refused to be taken, and the loss of hooks
and leader followed. A dozen times I made the
essay, and a dozen times the results were similar.
What those leviathans were, I never knew with certainty, but I always strongly suspected the ravisher to
be no less than a dolphin (*Delphinus Tursio*). To
possess a big fellow I found was impossible, so I
stuck to the little mackerel, and revenged upon them
at breakfast the next morning, the depredations of
their seniors.

At Catalin Bay, where I had to serve the allotted
period of imprisonment, I found the fishing even better than on the west side. When I was sent there,
I should have liked to question the colonel as to the
justice of his selection, but after all, the two months
flitted by, and even now I look back with pleasure to
the simple, small Genoese fishing-village. Perhaps
by chance there is a fisherman stationed there now;
well, if so, I will put him up to the ropes. As you go

along southward from the village to visit your guards, there is a cave. Passing through it you find a port-hole, looking perpendicularly down on the Mediterranean. When there is an easterly wind blowing, the surf breaks beneath in grandest splendor. From this port-hole, with strong tackle and plenty of fresh sardines for bait, you can take more fish in the course of the day than will suffice for your whole detachment.

Off Catalin Bay there is a bank, four good miles from land. Get the village fishermen to take you to it, and if fortune smiles upon you with the favor it did on me, you will cry before the night is over, "Hold, enough." The fish principally taken were a copper-colored bream,* about two or three pounds in weight, and so numerous were they, that we never thought of drawing up our lines till we had two or more victims hooked; and how do you think we knew this? Simply in this way, one fish on, you only felt a direct tug, two or more a constant vibration, as if a party were squabbling over the line, and each endeavoring to take possession of it.

* Called by the Spaniards "Bissengo."

SPORTING REMINISCENCES.

For some days I had had a terribly hard time of it. The ground had drunk its full—and to spare—of snow-water, game was scarce and wild, and the scanty herbage that my horse and mule were able to obtain since we entered the plains was barely sufficient to keep them alive; still, good seventy miles more had to be traversed before I could reach the friendly shelter of the belt of timber that surrounded the Fork. If it had been autumn, I dare not have chosen this route, for it is a debatable ground of the Camanche and Arrapahoe, to whom a solitary white man would be so tempting a morsel that he could not fail to be caught, and we will not say what done to; the very conjecture is disagreeable. The severity of the late weather, therefore, was my safety; for red skins, no less than white men, dislike unnecessary exposure. Still I was convinced some stragglers must have lately visited the neighborhood, for the occasional head of game I saw was so wary that I concluded hunters had lately

disturbed them. One thing was very much in my
favor—I was in the lightest of marching order, no
pack of peltries or well-stocked kit had I, for a
few pounds of bullets, a pound of powder, and my
buffalo robe, were all my animals had for a load.
How independent a fellow feels when all his worldly
goods can be summed up in so few words. To keep
as much in the nags as possible, in case speed might
be required, on the look-out for any thing suspicious,
with cautious, slow steps, I pursued my route to the
eastward. Nothing occurred to increase my watchfulness; in truth, I commenced to believe that I had
unnecessarily alarmed myself, when, crossing a small
water-course, on the edge of which was a sandy
margin, plainly I saw the prints where three
horses had lately passed. The forefeet of one of
them was shod—a good indication. Still they might
have lately been stolen from some distant white
settlement, so all my previous alarm and caution
were again reverted to. Half an hour afterward I
heard the report of a rifle; but, as there was a roll
in the prairie between me and the direction the
sound came from, I could not see who had fired the
shot. In ignorance of what was to be seen beyond,
it would have been madness to have ridden to the

top of the bluff; so, turning off to the right into
irregular, broken ground, the effects of the previous
year's heat, I hobbled my animals, and started
cautiously to stalk my way to some high ground,
from whence I might obtain a view of the surrounding country, taking care to keep myself between the
suspicious direction and my beasts. I had not
traversed over 150 yards, and was halting, the
better to notice the most available cover for future
progress, when first the head and shoulders, then
the entire figure, of a man loomed o'er the top of
the swell. Camanche or Arrapahoe I knew at once
he was not—perhaps Osage or Pottawatomie; but
what the deuce would bring them so many hundred
miles from their own hunting lands? However, as
every thing in the shape of red skins is to be dealt
cautiously with, I changed my caps and got into
most convenient and unconspicuous shooting attitude, determined not to throw away a shot, or,
much less, give my supposed foe a chance of returning the compliment. That he was alone, being
dismounted, I knew could not be the case; and as
he was coming in the very direction of my fresh trail,
which, if he was permitted to cross, he could not fail
to discover, and, with the discovery, bring his whole

party in pursuit of me, there was but one alternative therefore for me to adopt. Last year, in this very locality, the Indians had been unusually active; scarcely a gang of emigrants or traders who had taken the southern route but had lost members of their party; in several instances neither sex nor age had been spared by these blood-thirsty marauders, so what could I expect if alone I fell into the hands of a party of braves on the war-path? True, my scalp—for it has long been ignorant of a scalp-lock—would scarcely be worth lifting, but then I did not want to knock under yet; and if so I preferred making a fight for it, as, I think, under the excitement, the process of being wiped out is less painful.

By this time my stalwart apparition had approached within eighty yards; he was a noble-looking figure, without the slouch of the red man when hunting, and his step was as free and independent as if he had been shooting over a private manor. A big bug he evidently was, conscious of his own divinity, still no eagle's feather or characteristic mark of a chief distinguished him; presently he halted, and threw his large gun across his arm, when I saw at once that he was a white man. Great was his surprise when he saw me leave my ambush; quick as thought his rifle was cocked and brought to the port, but I prevented him **from** further hostile demonstrations by a salute **in mother tongue.** Our meeting **was** strange, both took a pretty good **stare, and then mutually** mentioned each **other's name, for we** had **met before, and** where?—**in no less distant a portion of the earth than in the realms of the** Tycoon. A restless spirit, **a crack shot,** and passionately fond of field sports, the world was his demesne—and where game was abundant, there he would **be found,** whatever were the dangers that surrounded it, **laughing at** hardship **and** privation, the bitters that make the sweets of life the more enjoyable by contrast.

Securing my animals, I accompanied him to the party to which he had attached himself; they had only lately left civilization, and through his interest **my equine companions got a feed of corn,** to which they had long been unaccustomed; the night passed discussing old friends, a flask of brandy, and a package of kill-a-kinnick tobacco; and when on the morrow I shook his sterling hand at parting, before recommencing my journey, he **presented me** with a couple more feeds of grain, which, without doubt, materially assisted my four-footed friends in rapidly traversing the balance of the debatable ground.

FISHING OFF THE CAPE OF GOOD HOPE.

Who has tried the fishing in Simon's Bay, Cape of Good Hope? Well, I have, and had such a take of fish as seldom do I remember falling to my lot. Those who have not visited southern Africa will please to learn that the coast is wild, irregular, and rocky; possibly as uninviting as can be imagined; and the waves that roll in on this distant shore, are giants in stature. Outside the anchorage of Simon's Bay is a light-ship; it marks the end of a most dangerous reef, which has pounded many a hole in stout-built vessels: but this reef, though repellant to navigators, is most attractive to the inhabitants of the briny deep; and close to the light-ship, on the edge of the reef, we dropped anchor and commenced work.

The bait, which certainly deserves a description, for such curious-looking shell-fish I never previously saw, was neither an oyster nor a mussel; it looked a little like both, for it had a hard external shell, and numbers clung together in bunches ; but oh, reader, hold your nostrils while they are opened, a description of the perfume is almost impracticable. If you have met a pretty little animal in the American forests, called a skunk, got a good sniff of his otta not of roses, you may imagine the other, being tolerably similar, only that there was the additional flavor of decomposed fish. But if we disliked the perfume, and made wry faces over it, the fish did not. They took it with a bolt the moment it reached the bottom. The prizes that we obtained were all rock fish, some of them of immense size ; in two or three hours we must have had several hundred-weight in our boat, but unfortunately it commenced to blow, and we were compelled to up anchor, and run for it. Weather on this coast is very variable, not unlike what often will be experienced in the west of Scotland.

From the ship some of the seamen took a splendid fish, both for table and appearance. By the bumboat people it was denominated the Cape salmon. As might be supposed, it had no relationship to the salmon family, but belonged, I think, to the same genus as the striped bass of North America. The two are much alike, only the former is without the lateral lines possessed by the latter. This fish is well known here, and I believe is esteemed their best for the *cuisine*. A wonderful place also is Agulhas Bank for fish, but you must be becalmed to enjoy it, no pleasant circumstance when you are either in a hurry home or the reverse. A calm away down in those ocean latitudes does not bespeak a level deck, no, quite the reverse, the ship heaves, pitches, and rolls with the long swell. All motions are combined in her action, and the yards, masts, etc., creak and groan in the most discordant complaining manner. No, no, far sooner would I hear the blast whistling through the shrouds, ay, and so fiercely that the boatswain's whistle only played second fiddle, than listen to the complaining labors of a becalmed ship in the Southern Indian Ocean. But about Agulhas Bank. A friend of mine, a really good and experienced fisherman, had the luck (if such it may be called) to have a couple of days' fishing on this distant shoal. Now this person had fished on the Newfoundland banks, and had wondrous tales to tell, but never aught like this. His belief is that there is not a place in the world to equal it as a fishing-ground. If this be the case, is it not surprising that some tight little schooners have not yet made it their haunt? The weather here can not be more formidable or dangerous to shipping than the northeast coast of America, while the traffic and consequent danger of collision is infinitely less; moreover, there are excellent markets within as accessible distances as the vessels have that sail annually from British and French ports for the great bank of Newfoundland or the Labrador coast.

A BEAR ADVENTURE.

In following a flight of ruffed grouse, which had risen so far beyond range as to have prevented my getting a shot at them, I came across a perfect brake of wild grape-vines loaded with fruit. I could not withstand the temptation of halting for a feed, for they had been touched by frost, which changes them from the most unpalatable to the most delightfully flavored fruit. The day had been warm for the end of autumn and I suppose the fatigue of my tramp, together with the delightful shade afforded, induced me to lie down, and, as might be expected under the circumstances, I fell asleep. How long I might have been in a state of oblivion I can not say, but I was awoke by my companion, a mongrel English terrier, barking vociferously at some intruder. After a stretch, a yawn, and the usual awakening actions, I turned in the direction of Prince to see what on earth had raised his ire and disturbed my siesta, when, judge my astonishment, I beheld a large bear erect, pull-

ing down the vines not twenty yards off, ignorant of
my presence, but occasionally casting a furtive glance
back at his angry assailant, who took precious good
care to keep beyond arm's length. Men become cool
in such situations, either from association or the power
of controlling their feelings. My gun lay at my side
loaded with number six; if Bruin found me out and
became aggressive, at close quarters, say eight or ten
yards, I was prepared to risk the issue; if he would
only move off a little way, still keeping to windward
I thought I might improve my opportunity by substituting a brace of bullets. Under any circumstance
my gun would be required, so watching the first opportunity when the bear's back was turned, I brought
my double-barrel close by my side and cocked each lock.
Many may laugh when I say I did not feel nervous, but
I did not, and remained watching with special pleasure
the enjoyment that my foe appeared to take in crunch-
ing up whole bunches of the luscious fruit. As he
worked farther from me my dog became less demon-
strative, only occasionally giving way to a suppressed
growl, which his feelings were unable to control.

First one barrel was unloaded and the heavier mis-
sile substituted, then the next underwent the same
operation, Bruin being now out of sight, still within

hearing; but the tables were turned; if formerly I was prepared to leave him alone, I now felt equal to acting on the aggressive. Giving Prince a little encouragement, he again rushed to the attack, and it is wonderful with how much more ardor, knowing that his master's eye was on him. Soon I knew the dog had nipped him, for I heard a rush, and dogs will retreat toward their masters, which brought Bruin full in view. As the distance was greater than I liked, I hesitated to fire, but the bear had seen me, and disliking my appearance, turned to make off, but the brave little cur was at his heels, and as I cheered him to the attack, he never lost an opportunity of pinching Bruin's stern, who at length tree'd to avoid the persecuting little pest which hung on his rear, the most desirable course for me he could have adopted. By the time I reached the spot the enemy had gained the first fork, not twenty feet overhead, and is it to be wondered at, that at such a short range, with not a twig to intervene, and with a clear view of his shoulder, one barrel brought him to the ground with no more life in his carcass than the usual death-struggle? My trophy was not large but well fed, and his hams afforded me for many a subsequent morning a *bonne bouche* worthy of a hunter.

But poor little Prince got into trouble before he
reached home. As I struck the margin of a river
which lay in my route, I observed a large bald-headed
eagle sailing about. Keeping under the shelter of
some brush I waited for a chance. My right-hand barrel I had reloaded with heavy shot, and, as the bird
passed about seventy yards off, I gave him a portion
of its contents, which was responded to by his immediately reaching the ground with a broken wing.
Prince, plucky with the issue of his late engagement,
made a dash at the bird, but caught a Tartar, for he
was seized by both talons, and, but that I came to the
rescue, would have been rendered useless for any other purpose than baiting a wolf trap. As it was, after
I had killed the bird I had some difficulty in loos-
ening his claws, and I doubt if my faithful little
mongrel had lived to the age of Methuselah, he ever
would have been induced to tackle another eagle.

FISHING IN MAINE—CHAR OR TROUT.

MAINE, one of the oldest States of the many that compose the Union, is, strange to say, less densely settled, less cultivated, and probably less known, than many of those that can date their existence no further back than ten or twelve years. The causes to which this is attributable are three, viz., the severity of the winters, the indifference of the soil, and the rugged mountainous rocky surface of the landscape. But where man is scarce, there look for the wild denizens of the forest. Here the moose, **caribou, and bear** are still **to be found, the homes of the beaver,** otter, fisher, and mink remain undisturbed, **and** even the **dreaded panther,** painter, or more **correctly,** puma, is not **rare.** Neither are fish wanting; **the** country is a perfect labyrinth of lakes and rivers, which swarm with various species of the salmon genus: but sad to say, the grand, the great, *Salmon* *salar*, the beloved of the angler, the *bonne bouche* of the epicure, has almost disappeared, for unfortunately, on all the outlets of the rivers, there are towns, and the inhabitants have long since verified the proverb of the goose and the golden egg. What Englishmen have done at home, so have their cousins done across the Atlantic. Englishmen and Americans, as merchants and traders, have been credited with acumen and foresight; such credit they may have justly earned abroad; but their policy in reference to their home fisheries has been totally the reverse. Let us hope that they will at length see the error of their ways, and unanimously adopt the means that scientific men have pointed out, for remedying and counteracting their past transgressions.

But let not the enthusiast run away with the idea that in Maine there are no drawbacks to pleasure, that sport is found without an alloy, for the pests of every new land here swarm, black-flies, mosquitoes, and sand-flies; but fortunately their reign of terror does not exist over six weeks. The first (the black-fly), which is about the size of a small house-fly, and not dissimilar in appearance, is a perfect cannibal, refusing to be driven away, willingly immolating himself in his thirst for blood, and drawing blood when-

ever he can obtain a footing, up your trousers, down
your shirt sleeves or collar, everywhere he will get
at his victim. Kill them by thousands, the pha-
lanxes apparently undiminished will return to the
attack; and even domestic animals do not escape. The
unfortunate cow that had been driven up to supply
us with milk, I have seen changed from a strawberry
to a black, by the myriads of these vampires that
clung to her; and, but that we lit a large smudge*
for her to stand over, I believe the poor old creature
would have died under the incessant torture and irri-
tation. But if the poor cow suffered, so did we, and
it was only by constantly lubricating the exposed
parts of our persons with oil of tar, or oil of penny-
royal, that we were enabled to stand the ordeal.
Fortunately, the black fly is hungry during day-
light only; like a respectable citizen, he early goes
to rest, and equally early recommences business.

Next come the mosquitoes; I have found the same
gentry troublesome in the Mediterranean, bad on the
Malay Peninsula, worse in the paddy fields of China,
but all these lack the 'cuteness and insolence of their

---

* Decayed damp wood, which burns slowly and emits a great
quantity of smoke.

Yankee cousins. If your hand is bare for a moment
a dozen will be on it; when up to your knees in a
pool, and fast in a big fish, both hands consequently
employed, your face and the back of your neck
will begin to itch—to burn—as if scalding water
had been poured over them. Nor were the sand-flies
deserving of better character, for though so small that
you can scarcely perceive them, their powers of annoyance are tremendous.* Thank Providence that
none of these wretches are made as big as the *feræ na-*
turæ, or else genus *homo* must soon become extinct. I
will here tell a little circumstance that befell the writer: he and two acquaintances were fishing under a
fall; fish were abundant, but space, on account of the
trees, too limited for so many rods, so down the stream
he started, and forgot, in his desire to beat the others
in results, the odious preparation of oil of tar. After
half an hour's scrambling through brush and climbing
over rocks, he at length reached such a lovely pool.
The first cast showed it to be alive with fish, and they
in the proper way of thinking. Soon the gravel margin had over a dozen beauties glittering in all their
glorious coloring, but the sun was near the horizon,

* Called by the Indians "No-see ums," from their minuteness.

7 *

and the attendant warned the angler that time was up. On joining his friends, long and vociferous were their peals of laughter whenever they looked at him. What the deuce was up? On arrival at the shanty all was explained. The black flies had attacked him when so immersed in his sport, that they had been unnoticed, or brushed off, making his countenance the most extraordinary-looking mess of blood and bruised flies imaginable; but if he did not then feel the pain, you may bet he did that night when warm in bed.

Knowing that such torments exist, why did the writer go there? is naturally asked, and as simply answered, for before he started he was assured that not even a mosquito was to be found in Maine. Afterward it was discovered that the visit of his informant had been paid to this Ultima Thule late in autumn. A dozen times conclusions were come to of sloping (not for Texas) in the morning; but the attractions were so great that the entire summer, even on to the end of October, was got through, the last two or three months so delightfully, that the self-sacrifice endured in June and July was more than compensated for; and never can be forgotten the beautiful weather, glorious sport, and free independent life enjoyed. The State of Maine being of considerably larger proportions than England and Scotland together, it is desirable that the particular locality should be mentioned. Seventy miles from the thriving sea-port of Portland, along the Grand Trunk line of railroad will be found on the map the picturesque, clean, flourishing village of Bethel; twenty-seven miles north from it Lake Umbagog. Here you have the last settlement, and by following up the Androscoggin River, which enters the top of the last-mentioned lake, you get into a perfect labyrinth of lakes and ponds, united together by brawling streams, only navigable by the lumberman's flat or Indian's birch-bark. On all sides precipitous mountains rise, covered with pine-trees where there is a possibility of their clinging, or immense bowlders, to all appearance ready to roll from their resting-place into the waters beneath. And here in this vast solitude, free from cares, we made our home, fishing or hunting by day, and sleeping such sleep upon piles of hemlock as seldom is enjoyed on feather beds (that is at the end of the fly season); for though the bears might growl around, the gray wolf give us a proof of his vocal powers, or the weird note of the loon come shrilly over the waters, still all formed but a lullaby to make us rest the better.

In fishing the rivers of all the wild lands of the

extreme northern portion of the United States and the
Dominion for trout or salmon, little or no sport will
be experienced by the angler until the snow-water
has run off; in fact I do not believe the latter fish
will enter a river that has not got rid of that addition. We got to our fishing-ground just at the desired time; a guide we consulted said we were too
soon. It being better to be early than late, we
pushed at once for our first halting-place, and the
result was that we hit things so nicely that we struck
the opening day. For about two or three weeks
the take was very great, and the variety of coloring
among our prizes something wonderful. A collect-
ing naturalist, a pupil of the celebrated professor of
natural history at Harvard College, Cambridge, Massachusetts, joined our party a few days after our
arrival, and all these various colored fish were designated by him as *Salmo fontinalis*. To so great an
authority I did not presume to differ, still when he
informed me that the *Salmo fontinalis* of American
waters was identical with our home brook-trout I
thought that the lively, game little beauty of our
mountain streams had wonderfully changed in color
and appearance from his trans-Atlantic brother, or
vice versâ. As the weather began to get warmer

the more brilliant-colored specimens became scarcer, and ultimately ceased to be taken in the river. This circumstance induced me further to think that there was some difference either in habits or choice of haunts which their more plain clothed relatives did not affect, and that at least there were different varieties, if not species, among the inhabitants of this stream; and the more I think the subject over now the more thoroughly do I feel convinced that the name of *Salmo fontinalis* has been frequently applied to what is, in reality, our red-bellied char. Memory is often not to be depended upon, but with the assistance of a few notes (the lapse of time not being more than three years), I will endeavor to tell the differences that I most particularly observed. In outline of shape what I suppose to be the red-bellied char much resembled a well-fed trout, except that the first dorsal fin is nearer the head, the caudal fin has a wider spread at its termination, and the junction of their caudal fin with the body is more tapered away. In coloring the back was of a deep mackerel green, interwoven with irregular darker waving lines, while the belly was as brilliant as burnished copper. Above, where the green of the back and red of the stomach ran into each other, there were three lateral lines of large brilliant red spots, interspersed with minor straw-colored ones, and in some specimens the anal and pectoral fins had the first two or three spines black. Altogether in shape and coloring a more game-looking, beautiful fish can not be imagined; moreover, their table qualities surpassed in delicacy of flavor any fish I have ever eaten, for the bright red flesh had a delicate nutty flavor indescribable, and, I fear, scarcely imaginable. Our guide, who was also cook and master of camp, used to fry in cream the smaller ones, and I doubt if ever prince or epicure had a dish placed before him more worthy of his palate.

But having given what I know to be, more particularly to the naturalist, a far from perfect description of this handsome fish's peculiarities, its habits, as differing from the trout I have known, may have interest. With the artificial fly they were not so readily taken as with minnow or worm. When hooked I never knew them to spring from the water, and the quiet reach of the pool was invariably a more certain find than the brawling neck. After sunset I never could succeed in capturing them, and the best hours in the day were from sunrise till it commenced to get warm, and the two hours preceding sunset.

After these fish had disappeared from the river, I discovered that they could be taken in the deep waters in the lakes, either with minnow or natural fly, the bait being sunk close to the bottom ; and the places where I was generally most successful in this fishing was where, our guide affirmed, were situated the springs that partially fed these lakes ; his reason for this statement being that this portion of the lake always remained open in winter, while the balance every year froze up.

Again, after these fish had deserted the river I had some admirable sport with them by going to the top of the lake and coming down on the annual lumber raft. I was put up to this by the guide, he for years had followed lumbering, and the rafts as they floated down, he assured me, were always followed by swarms of trout. His information was correct as to the numbers of fish, but instead of the trout of the river, I found my beautiful-brilliant colored friend. This habit is peculiar, to say the least of it, and untrout-like, and I could only account for it in two ways, viz., either the shade afforded by these immense logs formed the attraction, or the constant immersion of the timber in the water caused the insect denizens of the bark to be drowned out of their retreats, and dropping off in the water furnished these fish with a favorite food.

Summer drifted past, and with it disappeared the incessant persecuting flies. Autumn, with all that brilliant coloring so remarkable in America, made its appearance, and the oppressive heat gave way to the most desirable temperature. An English autumn to me is always sad, an American autumn is quite the reverse; the hues and colors of the former are somber, in those of the latter brilliancy unsurpassable predominates. An American autumn once seen makes as lasting an impression on the memory of matureage, as the gorgeous fairy scene of the pantomime when first beheld upon that of youth. For some time none of the bright-hued fish had been taken, and I much feared that my acquaintance with them for that year had terminated; but not so, a few sharp nights of frost took place, and going one morning to obtain sufficient fish for breakfast, in the run that formed the exit of the river from the lake, I with pleasure, in succession, captured several of the beauties. From that day forward they became more numerous, and the last morning's fishing which I here enjoyed, with the snow flying so thick that I could scarcely see my flies, I killed not only the greatest number, but the heaviest of the brilliant representatives I had captured during the season. With regret, having no desire to pass almost an arctic winter, I turned my back upon the three lonely, lovely lakes, with the following unpronounceable Indian names, Molleychunkeymunk, Mooscluckmaguntic, and Moligewalk, to seek the boundless prairies of the far West, and to substitute for constant companion, my double barrel, in place of my well-tried tapering fly-rod.

In my experience as a fisherman in Scotland and Ireland, I never knew of our river trout being captured in the sea. In Long Island, what is there called the brook trout (*Salmo fontinalis*) is well known periodically, when practicable, to visit salt water; in fact they are constantly taken with the fly in the tidal portion of those streams. The char of Norway and Sweden does the same, and I can only say that both these fish are wondrously alike. On the other hand, the brilliant-colored inhabitants of the interior lakes of Maine, that I have mentioned,. can not do so, for if they survived the descent of the Burling falls, their ascent would be impossible. Although the arctic char goes to the sea, the more resplendent colored relation remains, I think, con-

7*

stantly in his fresh-water retreats—*id est*, supposing
this is a char.   To me it would be particularly interesting to know if my surmises as to the proper
species of this beautiful fish are correct; and doubtless there are numbers of English fishermen whose
verdict, even from my imperfect description, would
set at rest a point important both to naturalist
and sportsman. *

  * Since the above was written specimens have been forwarded
to Mr. Frank Buckland from America, and the surmises of the
author are found to be correct.

ANIMAL LIFE,

" There is a pleasure in the pathless wood,
There is a rapture on the lonely shore. "

UNDOUBTEDLY every one who loves nature has
felt the truth of the above assertions, but is not this
pleasure, this rapture increased by the addition of
animal life, whether it be the occasional glimpse of
the timid hare, the momentary glance of the graceful
playful squirrel, the sea-birds dipping o'er the countless waves, or the fish-hawk hunting for his prey?
Yes, there is society, where man does not intrude,
and that society the most enchanting, that of the
beautiful wild animals, rejoicing in their freedom,
happy in their liberty, knowing no fear, dreading no
intrusion. For hours in the far western forests of
America I have stood, scarcely daring to breathe for
fear I should disturb some family party, ay, although
I knew full well that but for a successful shot, supperless I should have to sleep; yet who that could
for a moment think, would wantonly destroy a mem-

ber of the little coterie; disturb their innocent gambols, their playful, graceful tricks. Were they but for a moment aware of man's dreaded presence, all would precipitantly make a hurried and fearful retreat. The true lover of nature loves not alone the landscape, but loves those numerous additions, fascinating and inexpressible, without which, the effect of the grand foreground, the beautiful intermediate, and the soft subdued distance, would be materially diminished. In the northern portion of the State of Maine, the scenery is truly sublime; mountain after mountain rises, as if each strove to overtop the other. Giant pine-trees cling from precipice and crag, hanging as if suspended in the air, bowlders and rocks of all fantastic outlines, far, far above threaten instant destruction to all underneath; brawling streams, grandly impetuous, leap and throw themselves from rock to rock, while every now and then glimpses of glassy surfaced lakes, embosomed in wood, form a lovely distance. But this country, lovely as it is, is almost destitute of animal life; no songster greeted my ear with his melody; no startled deer bounded across my path, so that an intense solitude that became painful prevented the enjoyment that might have been anticipated. But if grand natural scenery, ne'er desecrated by the hand of man, wants animal life to set it off to the greatest perfection, how much more do our tame artificial grounds and waters require this adjunct?

Few of our citizens can, when they choose, fly away into the highlands, the lake district, or the wilds of of Connemara, but have to be satisfied with the artificial and formal beauties which our numerous public and private pleasure-grounds afford; but would not the enjoyment of those resorts be greatly enhanced if more animal life was added to the picture? In the city of Philadelphia a public park is tenanted by great numbers of squirrels, of different varieties, whose tameness, merry antics, and sprightliness cause them to be the admiration of all visitors. Could not squirrels be introduced here? not our common red variety, but the handsome black, gray, or ground squirrel of the American continent. What a suitable place would Kensington be for such inmates, and what a fund of amusement they would afford to the juveniles that in such numbers frequent it! There are also several beautiful varieties of water-fowl, whose advent would, I am certain, be welcomed, such as the wood-duck, sprig-tail duck, loon, sheldrake, summer and black duck; all of these species are ex-

ceedingly hardy, and the Serpentine and numerous
other artificial waters are equally adapted to them.
Further, while on the subject aquatic, I am informed
that there are fish in the majority of these miniature
lakes, but they must be of a very base order, grovel-
ers in mud, so much afraid to show their ugly car-
casses that the human eye is never greeted with their
presence; of course in comparatively speaking stagnant water, the river or brook trout would not flourish, the lake trout might, although I doubt it, there
being an insufficiency of depth without cool springs
at the bottom to prevent the water in summer becoming heated, and a cold retreat is absolutely necessary for their health.   However, there is a fish
across the Atlantic, equal to either of the two mentioned, gamer for his size and a much bolder feeder,
viz., the black bass, which is a frequenter of both
running and still water, clear or muddy, an admirable table adjunct, and almost unmatchable in the eyes
of the sportsman for pluck and gameness, taking indiscriminately the artificial fly or trolling bait, springing from the water when hooked, and refusing to be
landed till after a long, fierce, and protracted struggle.   I have killed a very great number of trout, and
also black bass, and although it was a long time before

I could believe that any thing of the size could equal the former, I have for some time been compelled unequivocally to give the palm to the latter. Now if we had this fish in the Serpentine, the water would not remain without a ripple; his presence would soon become known by his rising at the flies and otherwise disporting himself upon the surface. Who that has stood at sunset by the brink of some calm river, or the margin of some unrippled loch, say in the highlands, where trout are abundant, has not been delighted to watch the eager fish rising after their prey, and inwardly made notes of the size of each, from the amount of broken water displaced? When we have suitable homes to offer, do by all means let us have lots of animals; much room for thought is afforded by their habits, much pleasure from their innocent pastimes, and the influence engendered by association with them is certainly most beneficial.

STRANGE FISHES.

WHEN returning from shooting pinnated grouse in the State of Illinois, I came upon a party of farmers who were netting a pond on the edge of the timber land. This sheet of water was about two-thirds of a mile long, with an average breadth of one hundred and fifty yards. The bottom was composed of mud, except the southern end, where it was gravel. Only when very high floods occurred in the Wabash River, was there outlet or inlet to this piece of water; still, I knew it was well stocked with fish, for on a previous evening, as I stood on its margin as the sun went down, waiting for wild duck, I had seen the surface in portions broken into spray with the fishes' numerous pastimes, or energetic pursuit of their prey. With curiosity I stopped to see the result of the first haul, and well was my patience rewarded, for what food for study was in the results! First and foremost, from the size and peculiarity of formation, I will mention what the fisherman designated a "spoonbill catfish"—a name without doubt given by some one who knew as little about genus and species as a cow does about a watch-pocket. This curious fish was beautifully shaped, with all those perfections that characterize the salmon family, but projecting from his head was a muscular continuation about sixteen inches long, and six broad in the center, not unlike the blade of a canoe-paddle. This spoonbill was entirely separated from and projecting over and independent of the mouth, the lower jaw being in its ordinary place; nor was the mouth large. As nature forms nothing without purpose, of what use was this projection? My own idea is that it was a feeler, used in poking about through the weeds, decayed vegetation, and mud: and by its sensitiveness the fish was enabled to find his food. On handling this *rara piscis*, I found that the slightest pressure on this attachment appeared to produce intense pain. The skin was entirely free from scales from the tail to the termination of the projection, and was very smooth and soft, not at all dissimilar to that of an eel. For a trifle I secured the prize, as I was assured he was an excellent table addition, and my informants were perfectly correct. I afterward cut up the proboscis to satisfy my curiosity, and found it entirely composed of gristle, the surface underneath the skin being a labyrinth of veins. Afterward I saw, at different times, many of this curious family, thus proving that they are in no way rare; still, I have never seen them mentioned by naturalists. Probably it is exclusively confined to inland American waters. Further, I would say, the vitality was remarkable, for after transporting it home it lived for over an hour. The weight of the entire fish was probably about sixteen pounds. The next attraction noticed was what is familiarly known in that vicinity as "the pond fish." In color it much resembles the beautiful black bass, in shape slender but graceful; the placement of the fins is the same as in the pike family, but the head is small and not unlike that of a trout. It is a greedy feeder, and from its being uneatable (the flesh being hard and rank) is considered a great bore by the fishermen. Their average weight is from two to four pounds. Still another variety with which I had been previously unacquainted was taken, viz., "the great western carp" there called "the buffalo fish." It is frequently captured of enormous size—several I have seen over twenty pounds. They are much and deservedly esteemed, and are taken in immense numbers in the spring of the year by spearing; for as soon as a flood takes place, when the water is rising, they rush out over all the inundated lands, wherever there is sufficient depth for them to swim. For more than an hour one day I watched a lad, spear in hand, who had taken his post over an opening which passed under the Ohio and Mississippi Railroad, made similar to a sluice for the purpose of preventing the water in time of floods becoming dammed. During my stay this youngster must have killed a couple of hundred-weight. You must not imagine that these were all that were in the net. Sunfish, pike, pickerel, black bass, catfish, mullet, and turtle to a wagon-load rewarded the fishermen's efforts. In the end of the bag, I was about to place my hand upon what I considered a rare prize, when I was stopped by the rough intervention of one of the people, and the exclamation of, "You don't want to die before your time? If he bite you, all the whisky in the county won't save you." (Whisky is considered an infallible cure for snake bites.) This nondescript to be avoided was like Siebold's salamander, with four of the smallest and most awkward-looking legs; the brute was about fourteen inches long, and was there known as a water-dog. It frequently takes the fisherman's bait, who prefers to cut his line and lose the hook to becoming on any more intimate terms.

BUCK-SHOT.

For many a day I puzzled myself to account for the uncertainty of the patterns frequently made with buck-shot, from the same barrels, with the same quality and quantity of powder; at one discharge at long range, say eighty yards, every pellet would enter a disk of five feet in diameter; at the next discharge, for no obvious reason that I could learn, they would be scattered over the extent of a coach-house door; through the first pattern it would be impossible for a deer to pass scatheless; through the second the probabilities were all in his favor.

However, after much time, I think not wasted, I believe I have hit on a method by which the wandering inclinations of buck-shot can be curtailed and reduced to considerable subservience. For instance, we will suppose a ten-bore gun (the size I invariably used abroad) be taken; procure buck-shot of such a size that the barrel will exactly chamber four, that is, that four will fit in the barrel without using force, for if force be used their regularity of shape will be injured, and their flight will become erratic. Having thus learned the desired size of shot, make a cartridge of tolerably thick paper, carefully place your shot in layers of four each; with some grease reduced to a liquid consistency from heat, fill up the vacancies between each layer, and as the grease cools and becomes solid, place in each layer, till the cartridge contains sixteen pellets, when finish your cartridge by inserting a thin, hard wad, turn down the surplus paper over it, and fix with a drop of glue. Since adopting the above method, I have frequently killed wild duck returning of an evening from deer shooting, at ranges far beyond the reach of ordinary drop-shot; at the same time I would not wish a sportsman to imagine that I would purposely load with this cartridge for duck shooting; but that I made use of them, as my gun happened at the time to be thus loaded. I am no advocate for long barrels, twenty-six inches being the length of the hardest-shooting shotguns, for ordinary shot, I have known. But I have observed that long barrels invariably throw buck-shot the best; possibly the reason is that the missiles are then the less inclined to scatter, or that the friction with such large grain being less, the impetus does not meet the resistance presented by the smaller and more compact fitting grains. An American gentleman who for some months frequently shot with me, had a ten-bore gun thirty-six inches in the barrels, made, I think, by a gunmaker named Abbey, of Chicago, and weighing very nearly nine pounds. Such a cannon would soon have worn me out, but my friend was big all over and strong as an ox, and on the longest and hardest days, whether shooting snipe, duck, pinnated grouse, or deer, never appeared to suffer from its weight. Well this gun was an extraordinary performer with buck-shot; on one occasion I saw him kill a brace of deer right and left so far off that I hesitate to say the distance, knowing how skeptical many are on the subject of long shots.

THE AMERICAN TROTTING HORSE—HIS ORIGIN.

THERE is no nation on the face of the earth so thoroughly embued with a love of the genus *Equus* as we are; and knowing this to be the case, I trust I may be pardoned in advancing a theory which I believe not to be a fallacy, in reference to the origin of the American trotting-horse, and from what source they inherit that specialty, entitling them to be acknowledged the fastest animals in the world in that peculiar pace. But in case some readers are inclined to disallow this superiority, and dispute the point, that American horses are faster trotters than ours, permit me to state that across the Atlantic I have seen many nags that could perform their mile in harness in less than two minutes and a half, and three that have trotted the same distance in less than two minutes and twenty seconds; moreover they have the most enduring qualities, as can be attested by several having performed their twenty miles within the hour; and that, after much investigation, I have been unable to find a single instance recorded of any thing like similiar rates of speed having been made by any of our home-bred animals. However, it would be better to state before going further, that there are plenty of thorough-bred horses in America; but it must be remembered that they are all sprung from stock imported from this country, and that they are totally distinct from the family of trotters, although of late years the appearance of the latter has been much improved by judicious crossing the two,—in fact, so . much so, that some of the late crack trotters have quite a racy look, one in particular, Lady Thorne, who, if her appearance does not speak falsely, would make no contemptible figure on the turf or across country; yet from all my experience and inquiries I have been unable to hear of a trotting *débutante* of pure breeding, nor do I believe such exists.

Some Americans I have heard avow that it was the result of training, and that Englishmen did not understand the art of teaching a horse how to make such use of his legs, so as to obtain the greatest amount of trotting speed; and that they felt confident, that had they but the opportunity, they could select out of our pastures numerous youngsters, who, in course of time, would be made successfully to rival the performances of any of the prodigies who annually exhibit on the various trotting courses in the United States. To this supposition I beg to disagree, for I am convinced if such *rara aves* existed, their excellence would as certainly be developed in an English breaker's hands, as under the tutelage of a representative of any other nationality. At the same time it is true that trotting is not paid so much attention to, or nearly so popular among us, as upon the Western Continent, where it may almost be designated the national amusement; but what person of means here would not be desirous of possessing a horse that could outpace all others on the road, assist him to catch a train or post, transport him in the shortest time to distant meets, bring him home at railway speed after a hard day's shooting, or when thoroughly drenched, tired, and exhausted, with a long day's hunting in a heavy country, land him at his hall door in half the accustomed time? Doubtless all would like such a useful hack, and doubtless such an animal would sell at a fabulous price; hence the inducement, if we had the raw material, to bring it to perfection.

But have we the material? I say not, but believe our horses and the American (not alluding to

8

the thorough-bred, who are much in the minority in numbers) owe their origin to different sources, that trotting is a national characteristic of the one, galloping or cantering of the other, and the more I have seen of the two races the more thoroughly am I convinced that such is the case. In Kentucky, when visiting the farm of an extensive breeder, and who has bred and owned some of the most celebrated race and trotting horses in that State, I inspected both his droves of young ones, the race-horses and the trotters (for both families are kept separate and distinct), and was very much struck with the marked difference in their appearance; the latter being heavy chested, large limbed, small headed with tapering muzzle, while the tail was generally set on very low. However, if they differed in appearance, in manner and habit they were more essentially unlike: when you alarmed the thorough-breds, off they went at a swinging gallop; if the trotters, their favorite pace would be chosen, and in few instances, however much you might coerce them to increase their speed, could they be induced to break, and it must be borne in mind that the majority had not yet passed into the breaker's hands, so that their action was natural.

Again, I purchased a horse in Illinois, the produce of a very good trotting-mare. Up to the date of my owning him he had never been in harness. After a few trials he showed a very great turn of speed, and in a month or two was a very fast trotter; and so much did he prefer this gait, that no amount of punishment would cause him to break. Now, in this animal's education I did not use other means than those I have always practiced at home; still, I never previously had a hack that could drag a conveyance at the same velocity. To whom was the credit due, the horse or driver? Doubtless the reader will agree with me.

In temper and disposition a great dissimilarity is also apparent, for, as a rule, the American horse is very free from vice (kicking and biting being rarely found), sluggish, patient, and subservient, not unfrequently without a certain amount of mulishness in look and manner; in fact, one of the most celebrated trotting stallions (the sire of Dexter, who has made the best time in harness on record, and many others almost as good), is the most wonderful likeness to that useful cross, viz., between the horse and ass, and thoroughly dissimilar to any of his race that I have seen in England; however, he must not be taken as a representative of all, for few handsomer harness-horses can be found than Patchen, Jun., Butler, and George Wilkes, all three of whom have reaped honors which will long render their names famous among the patrons of the American trotting turf.

Having stated my belief that the transatlantic trotter has a different origin from our home stock, it behooves me now to endeavor to point out the source from whence he came, and thus in part account for the marked difference which characterizes him. The horse is not a native of America. If we may believe historians, on the discovery of the American Continent, no such animal existed there; the distant prairies and western slopes, which are now traversed by innumerable droves of wild horses, were then entirely without this genus. But whence are they sprung? How are these innumerable herds which are now found there to be accounted for? In the following manner:—The Spaniards were the first people to attempt any important conquests on the American Continent. The first horses that were landed in that country were the chargers of the military force under the command of Cortez. The natives who at first received the foreign invaders with the strongest demonstrations of welcome were overwhelmed with wonder, and awe-stricken when they beheld the strangers mounted on animals dissimilar to any they had previously seen. Nor were the Spaniards slow to avail themselves of this advantage, and in the numerous re-enforcements constantly forwarded, cavalry formed a large portion; familiarity between the natives and the dreaded animals soon reduced their fears, and as a natural consequence in many of the engagements that took place, the rider being slain the charger was cast upon his own resources and became free. Again, upon the line of march, doubtless many a foot-sore and exhausted animal was left to perish, but liberty and rest imbued him with fresh spirit, and the forsaken, broken-down steed, with abundant pasture, abundant water, perfect idleness, and self-control, soon became thoroughly resuscitated. Further, we learn that on one of the repulses which the Spaniards were subjected to, in their hurry to save their lives, they turned their horses loose, and took to their ship; and still again, when De Soto discovered the upper waters of the Mississippi, he turned all the expedition's horses free, as he had determined to continue his researches through that then *terra incognita*, on the bosom of the mighty father of waters. From these horses introduced by the Spaniards, introduced by De Soto, are doubtless sprung the countless teams that the traveler may daily see over the unpeopled plains of northern Texas and northern Mexico. The Spaniards then brought the first horses to America, from whence did they obtain them? None could be got nearer than Europe, none more conveniently than in their own country; we have, therefore, every right to conclude that the horses were from Spain, probably from the southern portion of it, as horses are more numerous there, and the inhabitants more partial to horsemanship. Who, that has traveled in Spain, if his eyes have been employed to take observation of more than the sierras and señoritas, can have failed to observe that the native horse is very unlike (in many respects) the English or French species, and that this dissimilarity increases the farther you go south; but it is in this very dissimilarity that the descendants across the Atlantic differ from our home breed. Moreover, in Spain I have observed among their nags, a great deal of what is termed in America "knee-action," a peculiar method of raising and placing the foot down, which is considered a necessary by the connoisseur in selecting an embryo trotter. The Spaniards like this action, they think it showy, and cultivate it in their saddle-horses, but for the purpose of display, they being too indolent or ignorant to turn it to better account. Further, the roads are generally villainous throughout the land, and very unsuitable for quick driving, in fact some of the most wealthy and aristocratic Spaniards, even at the present day, always use mules in their carriages.

The Spanish horse doubtlessly has a very large proportion of Barb blood in his veins, more especially those of the southern portion; this may be accounted for by the shortness of the sea passage which in the neighborhood of Gibraltar, in suitable weather, even before the days of steam, could be made in three or four hours; but the influx of Barbs into Spain, which must have been great, I do not attribute so much to accidental importation of individuals, as to the numbers which must doubtlessly have been taken there during the Moorish ascendency, for the purposes of war, more especially as the Moors at that period were famous as cavalry, and relied principally on this arm of the service for carrying out successfully their predatory system of warfare.

The Moorish horse also has very frequently this knee-action, previously mentioned in the Spaniard.

I was particularly struck with it in some colts in the neighborhood of Tangiers, and more especially in a horse, the property of one of the consuls. Out of the numerous importations which come to Gibraltar, I have seen several who could trot very well, and if pains had been taken, might have been made fast, not perhaps so fast as the American; but then it must be remembered that he (the latter) is a larger animal, of greater muscular development, which he doubtlessly owes to superior climate, intermixture of English blood, and the cultivating of this pace through successive generations.

In proof that the Barb can be made a trotter, it may not be irrelevant to mention that, when in Malta, I possessed a Tunisian horse as a hack. I ran him in one or two of the scratch races that frequently take place on the road to Sliema: however, he acquitted himself so badly that he, and I fear his owner, became quite a laughing-stock. Now, although this horse could not gallop, he could trot; and often surprised me with his spurts of speed when pushed. After mess one evening, a staff officer, who was my guest, kept chaffing me on what he was pleased to call my dromedary. To put a termination to his nonsense, I offered to back myself to

trot him to Sliema and back, from the St. Frances
gate, in less than thirty-five minutes. The performance was accomplished, and very much under time;
nor in the return did I push my nag, as I found I
had the race in my hands. Now this Barb, if he
had been in the possession of a person who would
permit him no other gait, would doubtless have become a fast trotter.

Although a great many years may have passed
since any direct importation of horses from Spain
to America took place, still the resemblance between
the two breeds remains most striking. The celebrated sire, known as Rydsich's Hamiltonian, whom
I have alluded to before, as the father of the present
champion of the transatlantic trotting turf, is unlike any horse I have ever seen in England, but is a
perfect counterpart of many animals I have seen in
Spain and Morocco, except that the American has
the advantage in height and substance. Few of us
have not seen pictures of the celebrated horse, familiarly known as the Godolphin Arab. Now, this
horse was doubtlessly a Barb, his appearance at
once tells it, if we can place reliance on the correct-
ness of his portraits; and even could we not, the
majority of authorities who have written on horse-

8 *

flesh, pronounce him to be so. In America I showed
a picture of this animal (if I remember correctly,
drawn by Stubbs) to a well-known breeder and possessor of trotting stock, and he assured me that it
was a most perfect portrait of the sire of several
trotting celebrities, and very like many others he
had seen.

I have further observed that a great number of
American horses were addicted to those most un-
gainly modes of progression called racking and pacing, a gait that is very seldom seen in England,
while in Spain and Morocco it is extremely common.
In fact, the Spaniards highly approve of it, believing
that it shows both horse and rider to the greatest
perfection; nor is the American behind him in this
taste, a good pacing hack being deemed by all as
the most desirable animal for saddle purposes. Having shown, I think, conclusively, the similarity in
appearance and proclivities between the American
and the Barb, and further, how I account for the importation of the preponderance of Moorish blood in
the Western Continent, I will endeavor to show the
difference between the Barb and Arab, how our English stock, with few exceptions, takes after the latter, and that it is from this difference of parentage we

may attribute the superior speed in trotting of the American horse over our home-bred animals.

During an experience in the East that extended over three years, where I had the fortune to see every variety of Arab, from the pure-bred Medjid to the Persian, I never knew one that was a good trotter or was gifted with knee-action; their paces are principally walking, galloping, and cantering, their movements being too close to the ground to excel in the trot. Nor can this be accounted for otherwise than from the great difference in the characteristics of the surface of the ground in Arabia and in Barbary, and that Nature with her wonderful forethought has adapted the gait of both races to the different surfaces over which they have to travel. If we are correctly informed, the districts of Asia, where the pure caste Arab is reared, is undulating, very sandy, and sparsely covered with vegetation; where the colt or mare can, without any fear of danger of interruption, lay well down to a gallop. But, on the other hand, Barbary is rough, rocky, and mountainous, intersected with ravines, and in many portions thickly covered with shrubs. On such grounds it would be impossible for a horse to gallop with safety, the velocity of his movements would certainly cause him to come to grief, and the better to avoid this he trots, his legs being all under him, enabling him to halt or turn to one side or other with the greatest facility. Further, by raising his legs so high in this pace he saves his hoofs from coming in contact with stones and brush, at the same time giving him a better choice of where he will replace his feet. Adopting this action through numerous generations has developed those muscles which are more strongly brought into play, causing a change of shape; so that if the horses of Arabia and Barbary have a common origin, their difference of appearance can in some measure be accounted for.

So far I have been alluding to horses as trotters, that is to animals of such a height as would entitle them to that appellation. For a few moments I will take a glance at their more diminutive brethren, the ponies. Who in our metropolis has not been surprised to see how they trot, it may be under the weight of a patrician youngster or fat butcher-boy, in my lady's phaeton, or a grocer's delivery-cart? Still they get over the ground at an amazing pace for such small quadrupeds, and much faster in proportion to their size and length of limb than their larger brethren. If we take up a sporting paper and see any trotting events narrated or predicted, it is invariably ponies that are going to figure, and wonderfully good time the little ones make, exhibiting speed, stoutness, and endurance that is truly wonderful, But where do the most of our ponies come from ? Devonshire, Wales, Shetland, Orkney Islands, Connemara, the wilds of Donegal and Antrim. Now on the coast of each place mentioned, portions of the Spanish Armada were wrecked ; a large force of cavalry doubtlessly formed a part of that fortunately ill-fated expedition, and is it not more than probable that many horses reached the shore ? If so, these ponies have Spanish blood, and by that link are connected with the Barb, their present diminutive size being the result of severe climate, exposure, scarcity of food, and possibly want of housing in winter. The wild horse of America has also become smaller than his ancestors, but not to so great an extent, from his range lying many degrees of latitude nearer the equator.

Further, all the above-mentioned places celebrated for ponies are rough, irregular, and rocky in their surface. Those who may be disinclined to acknowledge the Spanish origin or connection of our ponies may be disposed to think their trotting action is induced from the same reason that I attribute to the

Barbs, viz., Nature adapting them to a pace which is most suited to the surface over which they have to travel.

Now this can not be said for the American horse; the ground there is not stony and irregular, in those portions where wild horses principally abounded—the magnificent flat savannas or undulating prairies on either side of the Mississippi; so that it may be safely inferred that trotting in the American horse has not been the adopting of a pace better suited to his present home, but the retaining of a peculiarity inherent in his ancestors. This is a further proof of the connection existing between the transatlantic horse and the Barb, also an additional inducement for us to believe that our ponies have probably a large proportion of Spanish blood in their veins, and that from that source they obtain their excellence as trotters. I am aware that for some time great efforts have been made, more particularly at Exmoor, for the improvement of the original stamp of pony by the introduction of undersized Arab stallions. Success has been the result, and you frequently see ponies that are model race-horses, but, as a rule, the trotting proclivity does not exhibit itself in the beauties, but in the rough, shaggy, hardy, original breed, which not unfrequently more resemble mules, cart-horses, or even Newfoundland dogs.

In Australia, where racing has long been the favorite amusement, and where great attention has been paid to breeding, the proof of which is the excellent time made on their courses, fairly rivaling the best we have on record, I never heard but of one nag that had gained a great reputation as a trotter. Now in this colony a great number of Americans reside, and they, doubtless to gratify their favorite taste if they could have found the material, would have had some steppers whose reputation would have reached the parent country. Now it is a well-known fact that the horse is not indigenous to Australia, but that it was introduced from England. India, and the Cape—all three so far from Barbary and Spain that it is extremely improbable that a native of the last-named countries ever set foot upon her soil. In Australia there have been no remarkable trotters. To Australia I doubt if there has been any direct importation of the Barb. Englishmen have long acknowledged the excellence of their through-breds to be attributed to the Arab cross; at the same time, it must not be forgotten that many Barbs have been imported of which, as I have previously stated, the celebrated sire, the misnamed Godolphin Arab was one; therefore a great many of our horses have Barb blood in their veins, but it is in the minority, the Arab being esteemed the favorite animal, and consequently much more sought after when the foreign cross was deemed advisable for the improvement of our stock.

In conversing with many Americans on the subject of their crack trotters, and in what sires and families they found this pace better developed, to the English stallions, Messenger and Mambrino, many years since imported into the United States, they gave the credit. Now if any one will take the trouble to hunt out their pedigrees, they will find a stronger cross of the Barb (going back as far as the Godolphin and Barb mares) than is usually the case. Another stallion exported from here into Boston (Mass.), and who a long time stood in Long Island, near New York, called Bellfounder, or the Norfolk Trotter, has also produced a numerous progeny celebrated for this pace. Of his pedigree, although I used every endeavor, I could learn nothing; however, a friend procured me a print, said to represent him when performing the feat of trotting $17\frac{3}{4}$ miles in the hour, and never did I see a picture more remarkably represent an animal with the prominent Barb points.

To the difference in disposition and temper between the American and the English horse to which I have alluded, much allowance must be made to the varied systems of breaking practiced. The former, as a rule, commence to handle their youngsters at a very early age, almost making them pets, till they become so familiarized with man, that when sufficiently old they go to work with the steadiness of old ones; while, on the other hand, the vice which we frequently see at home results from severity of treatment, or from the teasing of mischievous boys, or bad-tempered grooms, who are too frequently employed about our stables.

A statement of the time made by some of the most celebrated American trotters I will here append, as it will doubtless be of interest to many; at the same time due allowance must be made that such is done from memory, I having unfortunately lost my records. Of one thing the reader may be certain, that if a mistake does occur it is only in the fractions of seconds. Flora Temple, one mile, on Kalamazoo course, Michigan, 2 min. 19¾ secs. Dexter, at Buffalo, N. Y., one mile in 2 min. 18 secs. Ethan Allen in double harness, trotting with a running mate, on Fashion course, L. I., one mile in 2 min. 15 secs.,

Dexter, his antagonist, being only two lengths behind at the finish, making his supposed time for the mile, 2 min. 16½ secs.

In conclusion I will state that I believe most thoroughly that the excellence of the American trotting-horse over ours is entirely owing to his having a preponderance or greater portion of Barb blood in his veins than our home-bred English animal, and for a proof that the American has this preponderance I refer you to his origin.

HINTS ON SHOOTING.

To lay down rules by the observance of which the majority of bad shots may become experts is easy enough; but the trouble is, however great the determination to follow the precepts may be, as soon as game is flushed the advice of instruction is thrown to the winds, and bang, bang, go both barrels, with the same unsuccessful results as previously. That more birds are missed by shooting too quickly, I assert as a fact that is indisputable; and knowing this to be the case, why will it continue to be practiced? For this reason, that many are so fearfully nervous that for the moment they have no control of their actions, or that they are so timid that firing off their gun they consider a duty, and the sooner it is got through with the better; neither of such pupils are ever likely to become crack shots. I have a friend who is, without exception, the most unlucky shot— I was going to say the worst—that ever I met. We at one period very frequently shot together, and each evening, on our tramp home, he was certain to tell me that he had discovered the reason for his apparent want of skill. How various the causes attributed would be beyond possibility of enumeration; however, he always devised some means of counteracting them —viz., by stuffing cotton in his ears, not to hear the spring of the game; to wear a loose collar, so that he could the better and more rapidly bring his head to the stock; to discard a waistcoat, for the thickness of cloth over his shoulder militated against bringing his gun rapidly up. However, he was always wounding birds—at least he said so; for constantly, if near, he would call out, "Don't you see the feathers fly?" which, perhaps owing to my less keenness of vision, I never perceived, save it were the feathers flying off with the bird. Another peculiarity this gentleman possessed was, that although he might have discharged the entire contents of his shot-pouch without bagging a single head, as soon as we both shot over the same point, one or other of the birds knocked down was due to his skill; doubtless companionship reassured him, or induced him to take more pains. I would advise such, therefore, always to shoot in company, only I would rather be excused becoming the company. Of course occasionally he would knock over a bird, but when this took place it either was lost or took no end of trouble to secure. I remember one instance in a marsh where we were snipe-shooting, a number of mallards flushed within easy range; following the report of his gun, one of the greenheads left his companions, sailed round several times, each circle becoming lower and less contracted, till he dropped. Half-an-hour was fruitlessly wasted in search, my friend would not give up, so I went forward alone; some time afterward he joined me, but his perseverance had not been rewarded. All that day he lamented over this lost bird, for, like many of our fishing friends, he doubtlessly thought it (because it was not bagged) far larger and far finer than any obtained. The reason for the so frequent loss of the few birds he hit was this, the victim seldom received more than a stray grain outside the disk described by the shot, and therefore was not generally seriously wounded. That there are many like my friend I know, and I fear it will be a hopeless task to endeavor to make them good shots; at the same time I think there are many bad shots who might be much improved.

I believe that too much importance can not be attached to the stocking of your gun. Occasionally you will meet with men who appear to do equal execution with either a crooked, straight, long, or short stock; but such are rare, and when found you may feel certain that they have possessed unusual op-portunities for constant practice. The length of man's arm, neck, and conformation of shoulder are so various, that seldom will a gun come up alike to different in-dividuals; the straight, tall figure wants a crooked stock; the short, stout person, the reverse; and inter-mediate figures, the bend between both extremes. I once possessed an excellent gun, with which I inva-riably acquitted myself creditably. The stock had always been an eye-sore, for it was composed of bad wood, and the previous owner had chipped and scratch-ed it so badly that, after lengthened hesitation, I deter-mined to have it re-stocked. However, when it re-verted from the gunmaker to my hands, I was sur-prised how indifferently I shot with it; but, on exami-nation, I found that the new stock was much straighter than the old. Again: being in a neighborhood where game was abundant, when I did not have one of my own guns with me, I borrowed from a friend, and my execution was so bad that before the day was over I gave up in disgust. This gun's stock was so straight that I doubt if any but its owner could use it. In having a gun made, there is nothing that should receive from the gunmaker more careful attention than the figure of the purchaser; for I feel confident that a very great deal of bad shooting is made through want of attention to this point. Again : a gun should never possess a superfluous ounce of metal that is not necessary to its safety. When we start in the morning, fresh and vigorous, after a good night's rest, the weight may appear a trifle ; but in the evening, if the day's work has been severe—more especially on grouse moor or snipe bog—you will be surprised how little tells, and will induce you to undershoot your game.

Still another equally important point is the strength that is required to pull your trigger. After long practice you may get accustomed to either very fine or very heavy, but whatever you are used to, that retain. With the tyro it is different. Through frequent experiment he should find out what weight of pressure he cangive without disconcerting his aim at the precise moment that he has obtained the firing line of sight. By imparting this knowledge to his gunsmith he will commence shooting under great advantage. A great deal, we all know, depends upon a good start. It is almost equally applicable to life, horse-racing, and shooting. If you begin under advantageous circumstances success becomes probable. Success begets confidence, and with confidence we are certain to shoot well. An habitually bad shot has no confidence. Constant failure makes him doubt his ability, his gun, in fact, every portion of his shooting paraphernalia. Nearly all persons who do not shoot regularly, fire their right barrel first. When such is the case, your left should shoot the strongest, as the second shot is so frequently at longer range. A good workman, however, will use either indifferently, and if such can be attained it should invariably be practiced, that one barrel may not be worn out sooner than the other. A fault which a great number are addicted to, is using too much shot. An ounce of number five, or any of the smaller sizes, is amply sufficient for a twelve-bore gun. However, if you have reason to use a larger grain, a quarter of an ounce more may be substituted. The reason for this is that the small packs the closer, and thus makes a more formidable resistance to the explosive power. For strong shooting, and, therefore, long shots, it is the driving force that is required, which you counteract by surplus lead, for friction is increased and power wasted in starting the charge.

Old hands may smile after reading the above, and justly say, "The fellow has told us nothing new;" but remember we are not all old hands, and that all were once beginners, for whose benefit these hints are given.

A CHINESE MODE OF FISHING.

In "Land and Water" is mentioned the circumstance, that while a pleasure party were descending the Thames, a large pike jumped on board their boat. The reason attributed is doubtless the correct one, but perhaps few of your readers are aware that in China it is a common practice to take fish in this way : viz., by inducing them to jump on board. I do not speak from hearsay, but have several times witnessed it, and will endeavor to explain how it is practiced. The boat used is built for the purpose, excessively long, narrow, of light draught, and close to the water. A board about three feet high and almost the length of the boat, painted snow white, is erected lengthways on one side or other, while on the reverse side from this board is attached to the gunwale of the boat, a shelf nearly the length of the boat, which gradually slopes to the water's edge also painted white. When the weather is calm and the moon bright, a single fisherman starts on the river in this craft, always shifting the board and ledge so that the former will be on the far side of the boat from the moon, while the latter is next it. The fish see the moonbeams glancing off this white arrangement and, why I can not say, jump at it, when they strike the board and fall into the bottom of the boat. On two occasions I examined the proceeds of John Chinaman's catch, and found it to be principally composed of gray mullet, and a representative of the Perka family. The Chinese, to all appearance, are a most stupid-looking lot, still they are wonderfully cunning in circumventing fish and game ; another instance of which is their training cormorants to assist them in taking fish.

AMERICAN RUFFED GROUSE
AND PARTRIDGE.

WITH but very few exceptions the grouse shooting for years has been an utter failure. Last year the results were the same, and we find ourselves thus early looking forward distrustfully to the future, hoping, but still doubting, that we shall ever again enjoy the sport which was usually awarded to our earlier experience. The grouse season for 1868 may virtually be said to have terminated, yet we are only commencing September, about three weeks' very indifferent shooting being all the reward the sportsman has received in remuneration for keeping up a staff of keepers, a large kennel, and, if not a proprietor, paying a heavy rent for his moor, possibly not only for one but for several seasons past. This is a dreadful state of affairs, enough to discourage the most ardent, for although he has paid liberally, still no returns can be obtained at all adequate to the outlay. The journey to Scotland has been so much time thrown

away, and the relaxation and pleasure well earned,
possibly after tedious Parliamentary duties, supplant-
ed by disgust, annoyance, and disappointment.

From the heather let us look at the stubbles. Nearly all accounts tally in the smallness of the bags made
and the extreme wildness of the birds. In this case
we have not disease to lay the paucity of sport to,
but a more than usually dry summer. Shooting in
England will thus be seen to be a very uncertain
amusement, for if the birds should survive the numerous ailments of their infancy, our eccentric climate
may still intervene, and however good the early pros-
pects were, when the time for enjoyment comes the
sportsman has to be satisfied, after hours of unsuccessful tramping, with the information that the heat
or wet, or a combination of both, is the cause that
so indifferent a bag is made.

If our game-birds are so susceptible of effects, that
shooting becomes an amusement that can not be looked forward to with certainty, the best remedy to offer
is the introduction of foreign game, hardy in constitu-
tion, suited to our country and the sportsman's wants.
In time these strangers might be influenced by the
disadvantages the home birds suffer from, but we
would have variety, and the season that was unsuited

to one species could scarcely be expected to be so to all. On the 12th of August, if the grouse fail, you have no shooting. On the 1st of September, if the weather has been too dry and the heat more than usually protracted, the partridges are so wild that indifferent sport can only be obtained. Now if the ruffed grouse and American partridge were introduced, if you could not fill your bags with one description you would with another, better far than returning empty-handed, disappointed, and probably out of temper.

The reasons that induce me to select these American birds are that I believe they are in no way inferior to our own, that they are extremely hardy, withstanding with impunity the intense heat of the Southern States' summer, or the protracted winters of New England. Many I know have objected to them, because in the wildest portions of that continent, where man is seldom seen, when flushed they will occasionally perch on trees, but this is not the case in the settled parts, where they have become acquainted with dogs and guns. In the Alleghany Mountains, New York, and Pennsylvania, I never remember such an incident taking place. Again, some assert that our country is too highly cultivated, which I deny, for the American partridge is only to be found in the neighborhood of farms; and I have been assured that this bird is more abundant now on the western end of Long Island, which is close to the city of New York, and more carefully cultivated, than it was in days gone by, and the country more wild. The ruffed grouse, on the other hand, but requires irregular ground, plenty of water, and a fair proportion of timber, and they will attach themselves to a neighborhood without straggling off for parts unknown, like the pheasant.

That the ruffed grouse will breed here, there is scarcely room for doubt. I know that the American partridge has already done so, and that in a state of captivity; but let the experiment be made—the cost at most would be but trifling—and, if successful, their importation could be gone into on a larger scale.

In America, over a great portion of the country, their partridge goes by the name of quail. The same delusion appears to have crept over here, and a fear that the introduction of this species would be unsuccessful, for the reason that our migratory quail is scarcer now than in days gone by, from the land being more carefully tilled, is advanced as a caution to those who might entertain an idea of making the experiment. The quail of Europe I know well; I have killed them in immense numbers in Spain, Italy, and Greece. Twenty years ago in the north of Ireland, when partridge shooting, I seldom would conclude a day without bagging several couple; so I have no hesitation in saying that these birds are so totally dissimilar, that what might affect the residence of one should not be entertained as an argument to prevent the introduction of the other.

THE POWER OF A SHARK'S JAW.

EIGHT bells had only struck a few minutes, and the old watch had been relieved, when the captain came on deck and ordered a man into the chains to heave the lead and obtain correct soundings. For several days this order had been so frequently given that it attracted little attention; and only that I happened to be lounging near the waist of the ship at the time, ruminating over a Manilla cheroot, I should not have been an eyewitness to the following incident.

The weather was thick, blustering, and wet. For a day or two we had been unable to obtain an observation, and as we were in a most dangerous part of the Chinese seas, it was necessary to be more than usually careful. Moreover, the barometer had suddenly fallen, a warning not to be neglected during the typhoon season; so our cautious old Scotch captain was not satisfied with bringing on deck the

topgallant yards, placing the ship under reefed top-
sails, but had as further precautions the lead hove
every half-hour. Although a long way off the coast,
the singing chant of the leadsman had in the earlier
watches proclaimed six fathoms, six and a half: shoal
water, all will say, for the center of a vast sea; but
for days between the Straits of Sunda and the mouth
of the Canton River you may sail without wetting
the knots that mark ten fathoms.

It may be necessary to explain, for the benefit of
the uninitiated, that the deep-sea lead is a bar of
that metal about two feet long gradually tapering
from the base (which is about four or five inches in
diameter) to the top, where the line is made fast.
In the base is a deep indentation, containing about
half a pound of lard, which coming in contact with
the bottom, informs the navigator (by the particles
that adhere) of what formation the surface of mother
earth is composed. The line which is attached is of
various lengths (a hundred fathoms, I think, was on
this occasion), carefully coiled in a tub, so that nothing can prevent it being freely paid out.

Well, the lead was hove, and rapidly the line ran
out; five, six, seven fathoms were passed, still no
stop,—on, on, till double that number, yet no indi-

cation of bottom. The captain looked surprised, but said nothing, till a third of the contents of the tub had gone over board, and then he uttered an exclamation very forcible, but far from polite. However this did not alter matters, for soon scarce twenty fathoms were left. The seaman was now ordered to stop the line, and in doing so exclaimed, after a violent effort, that he was unable. Two or three turns round a belaying-pin soon settled this difficulty, and at length the lead was drawn on board. On being handled, it was found to be very much cut; so, to have a better inspection, it was transferred at once to the chart-room. On examination we found on the reverse sides a succession of furrows over half an inch deep, out of which we picked, with the point of the compasses, a number of broken fragments of a large shark's teeth. The opinion of the majority was that the brute had smelt the fat and been thus induced to lay hold. From my knowledge of the habits of the fish, I believe he was attracted by the glitter of the metal passing rapidly through the water; under either circumstance, the rapidity with which he must have dashed through the water to seize his prey, is a proof of the agility with which some of the species of this genus are possessed. The amount of strength of jaw necessary to make such deep indentations on a bar of lead four or five inches in diameter, can scarcely be conceived possible in a cartilaginous fish. If this shark is still alive, I pity the sailor that chances to fall over board in his neighborhood.

BLACK BASS AND MUSK-
ALLONGE FISHING.

In the memory of the past there are always remi-
niscences the recalling of which give us the greatest
pleasure. Such is particularly the case with me when
I think of the scenes and events which I am about to
endeavor to describe. I was living on the confines
of civilization literally, for there was but one residence
farther north than the house of which I was an inmate,
and it was inhabited by a canny Scot, who never knew
what it was to take a day's relaxation, his entire energy, early and late, being devoted to the improvement
of his homestead. Shortly after my arrival I paid him a
visit, but I found that information on shooting matters
would have to be obtained through my own exertions,
for more than a complaint against Bruin occasionally
depriving him of a pig, he knew literally nothing of
the sporting capabilities of his neighborhood. It is
always pleasant on a new field of operations to obtain
a slight inkling of what you may expect. It is far from

agreeable to have to draw a charge of snipe-shot, and thus lose time, to substitute B B, or perhaps ball, small game being expected and large game found. The locality of which I am about to speak is at the extreme northern end of Lake Simcoe, where one uninterrupted forest extends northward for several hundred miles to the banks of the Upper Ottawa, except when an occasional lake or river occurs to break the monotony of this ocean of timber. In wandering about the neighborhood of my temporary residence, about two miles from home I came upon one of those beautiful little sheets of water so frequently found upon the northern portion of the American continent. This soon became a favorite retreat, for wild duck were numerous on a portion where wild rice grew luxuriantly, and wood pigeons and spruce grouse had adopted it as a watering-place, owing to its freedom from intruders. All devoted admirers of nature know what a pleasure it is to be alone where none of man's work mars the prospect, where every object the eye rests upon is as it came from the Creator's hands, unsullied and unchanged. As I sat on a rocky promontory to see the sun dip the horizon, perhaps visions of my distant land and far-off friends flitting before me, I was struck with the immense numbers of fish that kept breaking

the unrippled surface,—good evidence that the rod
and line might find abundant work, and on the next
visit I determined to put it to the test.

To those who are acquainted with the birch-bark
canoe it is needless for me to say any thing. All
the praises I could sound could not further enhance
it in their estimation; but to those who are not, to
them let me say, that there is not in existence a
more perfect piece of mechanism for the purpose
it is intended. Only learn to handle it properly,
and you can go in it anywhere, over shoals, down
rapids, through channels where an oar would be
useless, and finally, if necessary, you can take
it on your shoulders and tramp across portages
where nothing but an ox-team could transport a
boat. In construction they are models of skill,
yet the Indian alone knows how to make them; for
although a white man may occasionally attempt
their manufacture, they never do so successfully.
On the following day, with my birch-bark on
my shoulders, looking like a gigantic animated
letter T, I crossed the portage with a formidable
array of lines and artificial baits, full of most
mischievous intent toward the finny tribe. This
day the surface was broken by that desirable ripple,

whether it be for trolling or fly-fishing, and dark clouds occasionally darkened with their shadow the face of the water. With exhilarating freedom, deep I dipped my paddle, pushing for the rocky end, waiting till I had crossed the centre of the lake before I commenced to fish; for, as a rule, unless there should happen to be a reef, seldom any fish will be taken far from the margin. When alone in a canoe one line will be found as much as can be conveniently attended to, for the navigation of your craft requires both hands. Getting under good headway, I soon had twenty-five to thirty yards of line astern, with a few inches of red cloth for lure, which proved so attractive that I almost immediately had a break, and in a moment or two afterward a fish hooked. Of all plucky, determined fish, to Black Bass I give the palm, they are so thoroughly reckless in their efforts to escape,—first springing from the water, then possibly coming at you like a cricket-ball, giving you often more than you can do to get the line out of their way,—next dashing to the right or left, and only succumbing when exhausted nature refuses to do more. For two or three hours such was the sport which continued with never over a few minutes' cessation.

As I pushed slowly along the shore I came to a
river previously unknown to me, and which I have
since learned is the only outlet from this lake. The
edge of this stream was fringed with a dense net-
work of weeds, and the channel had scarcely a per-
ceptible current. On breaking full in view several
dozens of wild duck rose, conspicuous among whom
were many of the beautiful wood duck, a gem among
his brilliant-plumed race. What a pity at home we
could not acclimatize this bird, but I fear his migratory habits would sadly interfere. The sedgy nature of the shore here predicted pike, so, replacing
the red cloth by a large Buell's spoon with some
scarlet ibis feathers tied along the shanks of the hooks,
I again tried my fortune. Few who have not heard
of the muskallonge, the king in stature of the pike
family. He is to be found in nearly all the rivers
and lakes of northern Canada. Among the shoals
and rapids of "The Thousand Islands," on the St.
Lawrence, he is said to attain an immense size, even
eighty pounds; but the largest I have seen did not
exceed two-thirds of that weight. Such large fish as
the above I had not on that occasion to deal with,
but before I ceased, the bottom of my canoe had a
goodly show of bass and pike: so many, that I was

satisfied to select three or **four** for present use and hide the others, with my birch-bark, till I could send across for them in the morning; but **a couple of bears, judging from the** different-sized tracks, got at my *caché* during the night, and had the bad taste to maul and pull **about** what they **did not eat,** so that I rejected it as unfit for food. Fish **I have always** found the most tempting bait with which to attract Bruin into a trap, so I built a bower-house and hung up the **bait at the end of it, with my trap nicely cov-ered with leaves; still all would** not do, he and his **companion were too wide awake, or** had **left the** neighborhood. **This lake I** often visited again, and with equal success; the influences of weather never appeared to affect the fishes' appetites, and they are always a welcome addition to a backwoodman's fare. In company **of a** Chippewa Indian I also tried fish-ing through the ice. The method adopted is simple, viz., cutting a hole two or three feet in diameter, **over which is** built a small hut to keep out the light and **sufficiently large for** the fisherman to sit inside, the end of his fish-spear protruding through the top. **With an artificial minnow on a few feet of line in the left hand, and weighted so as to make it readily sink, you** attract the pike to the surface, when, **with a** dexterous blow, you drive your leister home. Very much like poaching; still where fish are so abundant and wanted for food, this system becomes less culpable.

At the northern end of Lake Couchachin, the beautiful Severn, after tumbling over a grand fall, starts on its erratic, precipitous course for Lake Huron. To visit this spot was not more than seven or eight miles of water, through a labyrinth of islands, and along the most picturesquely beautiful shore, wooded to the margin. Beside the fall was a sawmill belonging to a descendant of the French aristocracy, who had emigrated before the days of "The Empire." Whether or not the proprietor happened to be at home, a cordial welcome could be relied upon, and the fishing underneath the fall was always excellent—sometimes so good that your bait would scarcely touch the water ere it was seized. However, there was one drawback, for the spot was infested with snakes, particularly a large, thick, dirty-brown water species, which looked exceedingly venomous. From the indifference with which the mill hands treated them, I imagine their look was worse than their bite. They had, however, a *penchant* for minnow, for I saw one captured on the

hook.   As the wild fowl migrate this is a splendid
stand; for if the weather is in the least stormy, with
an indication of cold, the ducks keep passing all day,
and their flight invariably is so low that they are
well within range.   By following the Severn down
to its junction with Lake Huron, plenty of occupation can be found for both rod and gun; and the appetite your open-air life will impart will make all you
eat taste superior to any thing obtained in civilized
quarters.

LIFTING THE TRAPS.

On the northwest of the State of Maine exists a ridge of hills which divide it from the township of Success, in the State of New Hampshire. Whatever may have been the cause (possibly the presumption of the namer), it has remained as wild and unsettled as it was in the days when the whole country belonged to the aborigines. No, I make a mistake; a ruin of a tumble-down diminutive barn, on close scrutiny, may be found. The area of this township is composed of an immense meadow (through which a clear but deep and sluggish stream flows) and the pine-clad slopes that divide it from the State of Maine. For some weeks I had been residing eight or ten miles distant from Success. The person in whose house I stayed was a trapper during winter, when the inhospitable climate foiled any attempt at cultivating what at no season was a productive soil. Night after night with pleasure I listened to his stories of how he had run down

this moose, shot that caribou, or at length trapped
the most troublesome of bears.

For some days my fly-rod had been indefatigably
most successfully at work, furnishing not only my own
table, but many of the neighboring families with
trout, so that a change of programme was far from
unacceptable.   One morning as I was deliberating in
which direction I would go, my host asked me if I
should have any objection to accompany him to lift
some traps he had not visited since spring.   The trip
promised an acquaintance with a new beat, and an
insight into what I was not as yet conversant with
in this section of the American continent, viz., the
method followed of trapping martens.   As the sun
was rising over the eastern hills—for these primitive
people are early risers—we found ourselves about to
leave the surveyed road.   My friend bore on his back
a sack in which to place his long-neglected traps, while
I carried my trusty ten-bore double gun, loaded by
request with ball in one barrel, and buck-shot in the
other.   Our route at first was through a dense cedar
swamp, exceedingly irregular on the surface, while the
undergrowth was so close that it was with difficulty
parted; a thick coating of moss was under foot, so
spongy and full of water that if we remained station-

ary for a few seconds we would be over the insteps in water. Nevertheless, the tracks of the American hare were innumerable; an animal, by the bye, which I believe very closely allied to the Scotch mountain hare, slightly changed by climate and different habits of life, caused by the very dissimilar localities in which they are found. A blazed path was all we had for direction, but as both were in the full vigor of manhood, we steadily progressed. Several times we flushed the Canadian willow grouse, but as my projectiles were not suited to this stamp of game, and my companion continually kept informing me that larger might be looked for, I forbore troubling them.

From the swamp we got on drier soil, very rocky, and densely wooded with pine,— such glorious pine-trees as might one day form, without discredit, the mainmast of a three-decker.

Upward, like the youth who shouted "Excelsior," we kept ascending, but we had not the maiden to warn us, but whose warning I doubt not, unless she had been unusually pretty, would have been disregarded. Soon the walking became climbing, and after an hour's clambering the summit of the ridge was reached. Here the first trap was lifted, and at intervals of two hundred yards or so, according to the nature of

the ground, the others were found distributed. As
they had been down for nearly two months, whatever
had been captured was found in a decomposed state.
Soon the whole had been gathered, over a dozen,
when we descended to a stream literally alive with
fish; trout of all sizes up to a pound, appeared to be
actually crowding each other, while our presence by
them was totally disregarded. Lunch-time had arrived, and on the margin of the brook we enjoyed our
meal; several of the trout which my companion had
taken with the most primitive tackle, and rod cut from
the nearest tree, forming no inconsiderable portion of
the meal.

After a smoke and half hour's dawdle, we started
on our return, following an entirely different route,
still equally disadvantageous for rapid progression.
During our homeward tramp I learned that martens
could only be taken on the highest ridges, and that the
bait used was either a red squirrel, the beautiful little
cedar-bird, or the heart or liver of the American hare.
I was not a little surprised at the number of times my
companion halted to inquire if my gun was all right,
more especially as so far we had seen no indications
of large game, excepting some broken-up stumps,
moved logs, or scratched trees where Bruin long since

had been searching for insects or stretching himself. As the sun set, we once more regained the path, well fatigued with our rough and protracted tramp, myself not a little disgusted that I had seen nothing sufficiently large to be worthy of considering fit game for the heavy missiles which both my barrels contained; in fact, I could not help openly grumbling that I should have been inveigled into such a useless journey, to which I was informed that I might thank my stars we had got back safe. With this answer for the time I had to be satisfied, but that evening the mystery came out, and the selfish motives that had dictated my companionship being sought. I will endeavor to state the story as told by the trapper.

Last April, when the snow was on the ground, I laid out the traps we have to-day lifted. The traveling was very bad at the time, for it was near the break-up of winter. I got along the ridge all right; but as I thought the walking would be better to return as I had come, I had determined to retrace my steps. I had scarcely turned about when I found to my surprise, the print of an animal following my old track. I looked in every direction to see where the follower could be, but was unable to detect him. However, I knew well that the skulking villain was

10

no other than a painter (*Anglicè*, puma); and as I had only my old single-barrel loaded with bird-shot, I became justly scared. All of a tremble, I started for home, and you may bet I made tracks. The very evidence of the brute following me, showed he was after no good, and I was right; for as I drew near the outside edge of the swamp I saw him right ahead; but I went out of the way to avoid him, and after I left the wood I heard him howl, doubtless in anger because he had missed having me for supper.

At the time I could not help thinking that my host had been needlessly alarmed, and told him so, when he informed me that nothing would have induced him to return alone—in fact, that he would sooner have lost his traps than do so; that a painter in those regions, more especially in winter, was much to be dreaded, and in corroboration informed me of a little tragedy that occurred some years past in the same neighborhood. Two friends once trapped the township of Success. They had two beats, running in reverse directions, while the shanty in which they both lived together was situated equally distant from each. The one who examined the traps to the north to-day, visited those to the south to-morrow, changing their routes with each other daily, and always meeting at night at their common residence. Almost half the season had thus passed away, when the trapper who had returned for the night became seriously alarmed at the continued absence of his friend. At length the little cur dog who constantly accompanied the missing man came home alone. There is an end to every thing, and so there is to a long winter night; and with the earliest indications of day he sallied forth to find the missing trapper, whom he found dreadfully mangled and partially eaten. The assassin had been a painter. The tracks on the tell-tale snow spoke correctly. About thirty feet above where the corpse lay, an immense limb ran out at right angles from the parent tree. From this the skulking coward had doubtless sprung upon the unsuspecting trapper.

That the puma has attacked and killed human beings is well corroborated; but fortunately he is such a cowardly, skulking scoundrel, that he seldom makes the attempt.

STRANGE FISH IN CALAIS, MAINE.

THE strange fish lately caught on the coast of the State of Maine, and dubbed the shark dog-fish by some of the learned in those regions, I have little doubt, from the description given in American periodicals, is the basking-shark, for these reasons, that the basking-shark has been found on the Newfoundland banks not far from that neighborhood, that the basking-shark is the only proper fish with which we are acquainted that grows to this gigantic size, thirty-three feet long; that it could not belong to the whale family, or the inhabitants of that section of the coast, from their long experience and connection with the whale fisheries, would have known it, and given it either its proper name or a local one recognizable; and that from its being so excessively like an ordinary white or blue shark, with which the American coast abounds. To make the name more telling or characteristic it is christened with a Chris-

tian name and surname, each of different species of
the same genus. Don't laugh at the Yankee misno-
mer; remember the tunny that was melted down into an albicore by some of our educated fellow-citizens
and accepted natural historians. But still the most
important part of the mystery remains unexplained.
The anal fins of the basking-shark have an elongation
of a different color and texture from the balance of
these fins, which, if broken, would look excessively
like a flipper on a small scale. If the carcass had
been knocking about on the coast for some time before it was stranded, is it not very possible that this
fragile portion of the anal fins would get broken?
and hence the fractured members in the imaginative
minds of the country people, be supposed intended to
perform the functions of feet. It has long been believed that the basking-shark lives principally on ma-
rine vegetable matter, although on dissection one was
found to contain a portion of a mangled crab. In
my opinion a desire for romancing or attaching mystery to a strange animal has induced the good people
of "away down East" to exaggerate the most striking peculiarities.

BUFFALO PLAINS.

WITHIN the last year or two the borders of Missouri and Kansas, where they adjoin, have become so much altered, from the springing up of new towns, and the making of the Atlantic and Pacific Railroad, that the points which were formerly considered the best starting-places for the plains, on account of their being situated on the verge of civilization, are deemed so no longer. However, as in days gone by, I should choose Leavenworth for commencing outdoor life, if the intention were to reach the hunting ground by land. Although all frontier towns are to be avoided, from the number of loafers and blackguards that constantly haunt them, Leavenworth nowadays can scarcely be classed in this light ; moreover, the reliable and minute information with which you will be furnished by the ever-kindhearted officers of the United States' regular army stationed in its fort, is most desirable to obtain. But instead of going by land, I would by choice take the river route by one of the numerous trading-boats that sail for the upper waters of the Missouri, every May, from St. Louis. Here, also, I would purchase my horses and stores, which when once on board would be safe and well taken care of till required. However, to avoid the tedious journey up the river to Leavenworth, I should leave my traps and nags (provided I had an attendant), and go by train to Leavenworth. Of course it would be even better, if your party be large enough, and do not object to expense, to charter a boat of your own, as you would then always have a comfortable home, good hard food for your horses, and the means of transporting many luxuries, which it would be impossible to carry with a limited number of pack mules, for the river is navigable through a large portion of the best hunting range, and from the boats being of very light draught you can land or ship your horses without trouble ; on many occasions, while the vessel is progressing onward, you may be hunting, for the bends in the river are frequent and abrupt. The exact places where buffalo will be found is difficult to say. In summer they keep going north, feeding on the just-sprouted grass, up to almost the sixtieth degree of latitude, while in autumn their progress is south, till New Mexico and

Texas is reached; nor do they follow the same routes yearly, the section of country passed over one season often being deserted for years. A few years ago the Black Hills used to be a favorite wintering-place of the hunter and game, but it was ever dangerous from hostile Indians. All are now fled that locality, hunters, game, and Indians, and the formerly lonely sierras and woods now echo to the navvies' whistle, the stroke of the chopper's ax, or the grunting of the locomotive; but why I mention the Black Hills is, that between them and the waters of the Yellow Stone and the Upper Missouri the sportsman can not fail to obtain more game than it is possible to make use of.

RENCOUNTER WITH A BEAR.

In America a bear-story and a snake-story are synonymous, to the generality of listeners, to crammers. Knowing such to be the case a man can not help approaching this subject without nervous feelings, particularly when a bear figures as one of the principals among the *dramatis personæ* of the narrative. But it matters not, travelers appear to be born to be doubted. I do not hesitate to say that they will sometimes romance, but invariably the fiction portion is credited and the reality ignored. We do not need to look at the experience of modern times, our forefathers were impregnated with the same spirit; *vide* the reception poor Bruce received after his incredible hardships in Nubia and Abyssinia.

A friend, in the true sense of the word, and myself went to visit a small lake that was reported to swarm with trout, almost believing that no such place existed, but as a tramp through the woods was never objectionable we determined to make an effort to

10 *

find it out. An old lumberman, long superannuated, gave us our instructions thus: "First go through the woods two miles north, then incline a little to the westward, and after about half-an-hour's walking through a swamp you will strike a small brook, which follow up and you will certain sure make the pond."* To those who have not wandered through an American forest, such instructions will be perceived to be far from lucid; to the thorough woodsman, however, it would be sufficient. Before we left the township road where we were to branch off, there stood a shanty, at which we halted to put up the horse and buggy in which we had thus far traveled. From the head of the establishment we made inquiries, who, calling to his son, who was within, gave the following directions—" Bub,† take the gents and show them the pond." Now "Bub" was a most communicative youngster about fourteen years of age, and scenting a dollar in the distance, hopefully undertook the job. A cow-path we, the trio, followed for more than a mile, then we continued on what is familiarly designated a blaze road—*id est*, a path marked out

---

* Small lakes in Maine are always called ponds.

† A Yankee father's familiar way of addressing his son; daughters after the same manner are called "siss."

by a tree at every hundred yards, more or less, having a piece scooped out of its **bark.** The walking was as bad as possible, for constantly we were delayed by giants of the forest who had been **pros-**trated **by the gales of** the preceding **winters. At** length, tired and frightfully worried by **mosquitoes, we reached a** brook eight **or ten feet in diameter, but deep and sullen** as a canal; **down this we pursued an erratic** course till between two lofty **bluffs we came** upon a beautiful sheet of water of an area of **about forty acres.** To fish it from the banks **was impossi-**ble, for the sumac and cedar grew to its margin, so that no other resource was left but to cut a number of cedar logs **and form a raft. An hour or** more was lost in this operation, **and when we had** launched out we found that nothing but the smallest **fry could** be taken, although these were in such quantities that frequently we **would have three** or four rises to a cast. **For an hour or more we fished** indefatigably, **still** nothing over a quarter of a pound rewarded **our labors,** and when we landed for our pic-nic lunch I determined to fish the stream **with the hope of ob-**taining some heavier specimens. My friend, who felt indisposed, either from the effects of the sun, or some State-of-Maine whisky (which is warranted to kill **as**

far as a six-shooter), and which he had been imbib-
ing, refused to accompany me; so, with the youth
who had acted as Palinurus, I left him to ruminate
over his transgressions or misfortune.

As I had supposed, large fish were to be found in
the stream, and my basket began to groan under its
weight; when I hooked my flies in the top of a larch
that leaned over the water close in my rear. With
all my efforts I could not get them free, so sending the
lad aloft, I waited patiently for him to cast them off
The place where I stood was hummocky, such lumps
as you come across in the bogs of Ireland when snipe-
shooting, only a great deal larger. With care and precaution the hummocks could be traversed without
wetting a foot, but hurry would certainly get you
between them, when over the boot-tops would be the
consequence. I had stood for several minutes for the
youngster to get the line loose, when across the
stream, but a short distance off, I heard an animal
grunt; the spot from whence the sound issued was a
large clump of whortleberries, where some fallen
timber lay. Not being quite certain that my ears
had not deceived me, I waited, when the noise was
repeated. By this time my line was free, and my
juvenile companion was descending, when I asked

him to listen to the noise, for I felt convinced it emanated from no other than a bear feeding, enjoying his favorite *bonne bouche*, the blue-berries. Young America listened; Bruin gave another grunt of evident satisfaction, when the former—exclaiming "bear!" slid down the tree with such agility as would have put in shade the majority of monkeys. As soon as he reached the ground, off he started down stream, but the funniest part of all was that my guide, in the precipitancy of his movements, must have tripped over the hummocks at least half-a-dozen times in a dozen strides. When we had got thirty or forty yards off,—for I followed, though scarcely as rapidly,—my *amour propre* asserted itself, and I halted; not so with my companion; soon he disappeared through the labyrinth of shrubs, and I remained alone. To my relief I found no bear was in pursuit, so, placing my rod against a stalwart hemlock, I ascended its branches to take a view of the situation; for a long time I could not discover Bruin, but at length detected a large mass of black fur, accompanied by two smaller ones, busily employed feeding. They had quitted the wet ground and were on the edge of an acclivity, where the mother was most industriously drawing the broken fragments of shattered logs on one side, while her hopeful progeny feasted upon the beetles and ants thus exposed. The old lady had neither winded nor heard us, and she remained sedulously pursuing her avocation, perfectly ignorant that her industry and strength were forming a subject of admiration to a son of Adam. At length their search for insects took them out of sight, and I descended to join my companions.

The day by this was far spent, and neither of us having arms suitable for an assault upon the happy family, we determined to seek the settlement and revisit the scene on the morrow. Next day, at an early hour, with quite a re-enforcement, all armed with most formidable fire-arms, from the Spencer rifle to the old smooth bore, and accompanied by a well-tried bear dog, we sallied forth; for miles we tracked Madam Bruin by the broken fragments of decayed timber and the numerous logs she had disturbed from their original resting-place.

Finally, we thought she could not be far distant, and the dog was untied; off he went like a thunder-bolt, and in a quarter of an hour we heard him baying vociferously. Guns were looked to, the men most energetic previously now dropped behind, doubtless to examine their trusty rifles and see that the pow-

der was up in the nipples; but when we reached Watch, what was our disgust, of course, to find that he had tree'd a covey of Canadian partridge ?*
Unwillingly we went to work and decimated this unhappy and unconscious brood, nor could all our efforts afterward induce the unfailing bear-dog to take up the desired track ; intensely disgusted we all returned, and bear-meat and bear-hunting for a long time were subjects that few of the would-be hunters liked to hear mentioned by the residents of the settlement, for there was a strong suspicion that what was said on these subjects was said in chaff.

* Willow Grouse.

IDEAS ON FLY-FISHING.

To those who have gained skill from constant practice in the gentle art, I do not address my remarks;
still they can read if they will, provided they will
do so in good temper, and furnish beginners with
such minutiæ as have been forgotten, or have not
been told. I fancy I hear numbers dissenting from
my proviso, for it was only through long months,
ay, years of toil—we may also say pleasure—they
gained the information on fly-fishing which they
now possess, and, therefore, why impart the result
of their study to Tom, Dick, and Harry. But if
our forefathers through generations had held back
their views and experiences, for such selfish reasons,
do you suppose the machinist, the naturalist, the
navigator, etc., etc., of the days in which we live,
would be as proficient as they are in their respec-
tive trades or sciences? For all Izaak Walton states,
I much fear the followers of the rod and line possess the quality of selfishness. As one of its votaries,

I can well remember keeping buried in my own bosom, the position of pools, the color of flies, etc., where I was either certain of taking the largest fish, or by the using of which, I could almost guarantee myself good sport. But I trust I no longer possess this love of self, and in no better way can I prove it than by endeavoring to teach the young idea, not how to shoot, but to fish; come forward ye, also, who have experience, and help me in my task.

But to commence, we will first allude to the implements. The fly rod, like the gun, can not be too light, as long as it possesses the requisite strength. This is even a greater desideratum in the former than in the latter, for there is no convenient resting-position in which you can carry it incessantly; while on the river it is at work, not even the respite for loading being necessary, and if a heavy gun after a hard day's work will make you undershoot your game, a heavy rod will make you a sluggard at evening in striking your fish, and the result will be about similar in both instances. For the trout fisherman, he, I mean, who fly-fishes burns and rivers, from twelve to thirteen feet is quite sufficient length for his rod to be (lake fishermen frequently use longer, but what they gain in reach they lose in quickness, a loss, in my estimation, of most serious importance), and such an implement should not exceed in weight eight or nine ounces. I can imagine I see many cast up their eyes and exclaim, that such is impossible to procure, but let me say they are mistaken. I have owned several of that weight, and with them, days in succession, taken baskets of fish, of not only all the ordinary sizes, but on one occasion I killed a trout nine pounds in weight. As I can not help regarding this as a performance to be proud of, I will relate how it took place. A couple of companions and myself were encamped on the margin of Mad River in Oxford County, State of Maine. Our guns had failed to provide dinner, so taking a hazel wand I essayed to capture sufficient chub to make a *chowder*, a description of *omnium gatherum* stew. In taking a small fish, as I was about lifting him into the canoe a large trout rushed from underneath the birch-bark, seized the chub, and although I gave him both line and time to pouch what had not been intended for a bait, on taking a pull upon him the chub came away, and I was free from the larger antagonist. Having taken sufficient small fry I went home, brooding over my misfortune, but keeping the adventure closely locked in my own bosom (selfishness again). About the hour that the sun began to dip behind the giant pines, I had made up my mind to the course I would pursue, which was to take my pet rod, mount a cast of two flies, and carefully whip the hole from end to end. As if it were but yesterday, I remember distinctly the flies. The trail one was ginger-colored cock's hackle, with light corn crake wing, tipped with silver; the dropper a large-sized moth.

"For work at that hour," I hear some internally mutter, "the moth did the business." No, it did not; cock's hackles of all shades may invariably be backed against the field, and the cock's hackle on this occasion kept up its reputation. Down on my knees in the bow of the canoe, the camp-keeper holding her back by a pole in the stern, slowly and cautiously I fished the throat, from thence down into the less angry but wider-spread current, when just as my flies passed over an eddy that divided the downward flow from the back water, there was a splash rapidly responded to by a nervous quick movement of the wrist, which planted the hook firmly home. I doubt if I exaggerate, in fact I think I scarcely state enough, when I say that thirty minutes elapsed before my trophy could sufficiently endure the sight of a landing-net to have it placed under him. Thus

was taken the largest river (*salmo fario*) trout
I ever caught. But to my rod; it was made out of
cedar from butt to tip, did not exceed nine ounces,
and was the most lively, quick, light casting treasure
I ever used. Cedar fly-rods I have heard objected to,
because they are brittle; doubtless you may find
them so, and your casting-line also, if you change its
use into that of a carriage whip. However much
I admire a cedar rod I do not think it suited for a
tyro, but when the beginner has gained experience,
and is able to offer an opinion and use a fly rod as it
should be used, I doubt not he will perfectly agree
with me. A cedar rod can seldom be purchased ready
made, as tradesmen dislike the job; so if any readers of "Gun, Rod, and Saddle" should wish to possess
one, he had better go to the very best workman he
knows of, and give him the order.

Next to the cedar rod, but one that will stand any
amount of fair work, is the split bamboo; this, I
think, can be procured even lighter than the former.
There is a firm, the Messrs. Clark, of Maiden Lane,
New York, who make this a *spécialité*. I never had
the fortune to use one, but have handled them often
and listened to the raptures of experts on their merits;
on their good qualities I believe I can say nothing

that they do not deserve, but their price is necessarily high, from the care with which the cane has to be selected and put together.

When I was a boy, I believed Flint and Martin Kelly, both of Dublin, before all other makers. I have used their rods over a great portion of England, Scotland, and Ireland, and did not, until I used the cedar rod, believe that any rod ever was made that could compete with theirs, but so it is, and so it will continue to be. Old bluff-bowed lumbering packet-ships sufficed our fathers to go to India; now we have the P. and O. service, with rail across the Isthmus, and it is far from probable that this means of transit will always suit our children. If Joe Manton was to arise among us, I doubt much if he could hold his own among modern gunmakers.

Some persons, particularly Irish fishermen, are attached to double-action rods; that is, rods which have so much elasticity in them, that they display two movements, one up and the other down, when suddenly used. I do not like them, for more than one reason; the movement of the wrist in striking the fish, while raising the butt, throws the tip down, thus giving quite a contrary motion to what is intended. Again, if you have to fish against the wind, they will not only be found most difficult to manage, but excessively fatiguing. There is a rod made in Castle Connell (principally for salmon), after the above pattern; it has many admirers, who doubtless through experience have become proficient in its use; still I can speak only from what I know, and my verdict is, leave them to their present advocates.

A combination-rod has always been my horror. I mean such as fishing-tackle shop proprietors guarantee to be both a perfect fly and bait rod only by altering the tip. If persons will but use their brains they can in a moment see that such is impossible. The two uses are essentially different, requiring the spring and elasticity in totally different parts. The act of placing a dull, lumbering tip on the first three joints of a delicate, pliant trout rod is really desecration. However, some may say, you will find a medium between the two more generally useful. My answer is, what is worth doing is worth doing well; and if your intent is fly-fishing, the most perfect rod for that purpose should be selected. If the river is so discolored or swollen that bait has to be resorted to, or you must go supperless to bed, for goodness' sake go and cut a hazel wand, unless you carry a bait rod—an article for capturing trout that no true fisherman ought to be proud of. In fact, I am not certain that its possession should not entitle the owner to be arrested, in the same way as a pocketful of snares for game would a known poacher. Hybrids, whether in rod or gun, are to be carefully avoided. I remember being once entrapped into using a hybrid gun, in the township of Markham, Upper Canada. Going through some brush I flushed a quantity of woodcock. I stated the circumstance when I returned to the farm-house where I was residing. As I had no gun with me the host offered me the use of his, which from his description was worthy of a royal duke and therefore I accepted the offer. On production it proved to be half shot-gun, half rifle—that is, the right-hand barrel was smooth, the left rifled. This was my first experience of such a weapon, and most probably my last. The game was found, the cover was close, and snap shooting necessary. It was of no use. The gun would not come up, or the game come down. The fact was, that the shot barrel was only half the weight of the rifled, consequently the whole fabric was without balance, and do what I would my aim was invariably disconcerted.

Of the joints used in fly-rods the plain sliding one is probably the most convenient. If properly fitted it should never jam or work loose; but if I lived on a river I should never make use of any other than the simple splice, for the lashing affects less the action of the spring; and if a few additional moments are lost in putting it together, the return is ample recompense. But I fear the age is too fast· for its adoption.

Having given my thoughts upon the rod I will now go to the reel. Of late years, at least since I was a boy, all kinds of mechanical inventions and appliances have been used to produce a more perfect reel: there are now to be obtained stop reels, multiplying reels, and reels with as many internal cog and other wheels as would start a clockmaker. Of these complicated apparatuses beware, for they are fraught with disappointment and vexation of spirit; the old simple click reel is the only one that deserves the honor of being attached to a fly-rod. Still, too much care and attention can not be devoted to their construction. Every screw and joint should be as perfectly finished as those of a gun from a first-class manufacturer. The barrel of the reel should be wide in proportion to its length, for you thus gain power or give line with greater freedom; nothing is more unsightly or more awkward than a long narrow-barreled reel. Brass is the metal usually employed for their construction, but the newly-invented aluminium bronze is infinitely to be preferred, for it does not corrode or discolor with the action of the atmosphere, and it is less liable to suffer from a blow or a fall; mischances that the fly-fisher's paraphernalia, more particularly in a rocky mountainous country, are especially liable to when following the course of a trout brook, for stones will be slippery and of treacherous foundation. Who among our expert salmon or trout fishermen can not remember having obtained a frightful cropper when precipitously following up or down stream a heavy fish he was fast to? I do not require to tax my memory greatly to recall half-a-dozen such casualties.

There are various methods of attaching the reel to the rod. Of none do I approve so highly as that by which the reel is held fast in a shallow indentation by a movable band. In those cases where the butt is pierced, or the reel held on the rod by a brass band attached to it, which closes with a screw, the nuts are constantly getting lost or loose, through the thread being worn out; moreover, the hand not unfrequently gets chafed by coming in contact with them.

On the subject of fly-lines there is great diversity
11

of opinion. Of whatever materials they are composed they should taper. Hair and silk I was at one time much in favor of; but, after a lengthened trial, I found one great objection—the two materials had not the same amount of elasticity, so that a heavy strain would bear more severely on one than on the other, which ultimately caused brittleness. A plaited-silk line, which has been submitted to a process of varnishing, rendering it impervious to water, will, I think, do the greatest amount of work and throw the greatest length of line; but for delicate, light, fine fishing, nothing I know of can surpass the old-fashioned one, composed entirely of horse-hair; for they are possessed of more vitality, elasticity, and quickness. In the selection of one of these every foot should be carefully examined and tested, for a careless, slop-shop workman will frequently work in short and worthless hair, possibly in the center, which will destroy the whole fabric ; for if the line be once broken it is useless. It matters not how much ingenuity and time you spend over the splice. For a day or two it may pass through the rings, but the friction will wear it rough, and it will catch, sooner or later, not improbably with a large fish, for then the strain is greatest. Can any thing more disgusting

be imagined than taking the last look at eight or
ten yards of your line, perhaps more, rapidly disappearing in the eddying stream with your casting line and flies acting as advance guard? The
thought of such a catastrophe is enough to make a
man's blood run cold.

Casting lines should also taper, and, provided the
gut is good, can scarcely have too fine a termination. Although a great many disciples of the rod
always purchase these ready-made, every fisherman
should be able to knot one up himself. The process
is simple. Select your hairs—coarse ones for the
top, fine ones for the bottom—steep them for some
minutes in water, as warm as the hand can conveniently bear, then knot them together, increasing or
diminishing gradually in size according to the end
you have commenced at. Care must be taken
that such a knot be used as there is no slip to.
The safest I know of is formed thus: take the ends
to be joined and place them alongside one another,
then take one end and make a single hitch by doubling it back and passing the end through the loop,
which pull tight. Do the same with the reverse end,
when by pulling on the line both will slip together,
the strain having the tendency to tighten the knot.

After cutting off the surplus ends a few turns of very fine silk to whip them down and the smallest quantity of varnish, will add much to the appearance of the line. There is no amusement that I know of in which it is so requisite for the follower of it to know how to make use of his hands and his ingenuity. Bad luck, or whatever you choose to call it, may, before an hour's fishing be done, reduce you to the alternative of either ceasing work or manufacturing out of broken fragments a new casting line. Very possibly this is caused by the fish being more than usually on the feed. How disagreeable to be compelled to halt!—better far to spend ten minutes with the dry end of gut in your mouth, the more rapidly to render the hairs fit for knotting, and to know how to put them together afterward.

The rings upon your rod should be large and not too numerous, five are sufficient for the lower joints, and about five more for the tip, supposing it to be a rod thirteen feet in length, and in three pieces. In America I lately saw rods ringed on both sides, so that if after unusual hard work and constant use a tendency to warp was evinced, you altered your reel to the reverse side and thus counteracted it. However, the better plan, I should say, would be to use the reverse sides day about. The only objection to this double arrangement of rings is additional weight, but that must be very trifling.

Having now described the rod, the reel, the line, and the cast, I approach a subject that I hesitate to touch, viz., fly-tying, for I do not believe that any one can become an expert, but through constant practice, after having received a few elementary lessons from an adept. I believe I can tie a fair fly; but how long do you suppose it was before I reached my present excellence? Years; and even now I discover wrinkles and new methods of which I was not previously aware; however, one rule may be laid down: never to take a turn of the silk round your hook without purpose, or without giving it sufficient strength to keep it in its place and perform the duty intended. The most important part is the simplest and first, the securing of the gut to the shank of the hook. Unless this is attended to all your labor is vain and worthless—so much time thrown away and wasted. Here comes all the strain, and a thoughtless turn or two will cause naught but disappointment. Some anglers, particularly Irish ones, place the wings on so that the feather points from the hook, then double them back and tie them down. In this method much practice is necessary to form a handsome head; but its advocates claim for it strength. However, I have so frequently found the silk slip, and the feathers consequently point in the reverse direction, that I unhesitatingly condemn the practice. To make a handsome and serviceable fly, I have always followed the method of putting the wings on separately, care being taken not to injure the pile of the feathers; and this should be done last, the most minute drop of varnish being used over the silk when the head is finished off. My first effort to tie a fly turned out a thing like a humming-bird, my second like a humble-bee, and so on till I have succeeded in making a good imitation of a gnat. Patience and perseverance have done this, and none will ever excel in fly-tying without exercising these qualities, so essentially useful in every walk in life. As a rule, the bigger the river, the more water it contains; and the more boisterous the weather, the larger the flies that are used; but in summer, when the streams and burns have become clear and low, the smallest sizes must be resorted to, thrown with the lightest line, from the most unobservable and most sheltered position.

Three flies, their coloring and component parts,

that I have found successful on almost all waters and
at every portion of the open season, I will describe;
in fact, I have so much faith in them that I invariably use all three in making my first essay on an unknown river, viz., the red hackle, hare's ear and yellow, and black hackle. In America, on the small
trout-brooks, I found them equally attractive, evidence of a similarity of taste in fish on the Eastern
and Western continents. Fly No. 1, the red hackle,
body composed of rufus wool, twisted in with tying
silk, lower portions of body to be fine, gradually increasing in thickness till the shoulder is reached.
Shoulder of bright-red cock's hackle, the color that
is obtained in a natural state from the domestic
fowl, game fowls generally producing the finest;
but if those from the East Indian jungle-cock can be
obtained, you will possess the very best. Wings
put on separately, and obtained from the wings of the
corn crake, shot immediately previous to their autumnal migration. Fly No. 2, hare's ear and yellow;
this has a tail composed of two strands from the
larger feathers of the guinea fowl, body composed of
the fine mottled hair off the ears of a hare, mixed
with fine mohair, of any of the intermediate shades
from straw color to olive. The mohair should be cut

short, so that it will the better mix with the hare's
ear. This dubbing must also be tied in with the silk,
and the fly should be large at the shoulder. No
hackle in this specimen is required. The wings from
the large wing-feathers of the fieldfare, each placed
on separately. Fly No. 3, black hackle; body of blue
wool or mohair, finished at termination with a couple
of turns of silver tinsel, black hackle from domestic
fowl for shoulder, with the wing composed of the
feather either from tail or wing of the water-hen.
The angler had better be provided with various sizes
of these, as rivers are not always in the same condition, and weather is variable. For me to say that
other flies will not kill better on some rivers, or at
least equally well, would be absurd, but those described I have found most generally useful. A handsome and frequently very killing fly at times, particularly in blustering weather, is made of the following
material. Body of two of the longest and most rufus
strands of a feather from a brown turkey; these
strands to have the fingers pulled up them, so as to
cause the fine edges to stand out; then wrapped firmly on. Shoulder of brown cock's hackle, with brown
grouse feather for wing. In autumn, particularly if
the stream should be clearing after a flood, I have

known this fly to be most effective. However, it is
no bad plan if you are a stranger in a neighborhood,
to get hold of a poor honest disciple of Izaak Walton,
who will give you information, and very probably sell
you some of the contents of his book. However, be
ware that he does not palm off upon you the *débris*
of his collection. Except for sea-trout fishing, the brilliant and many-colored macaw-like compositions are
totally useless in our inland streams, so let not love of
gaudy coloring or the advice of inexperienced persons
induce you to spend your time and money on such
fabrications.

We will suppose the novice accoutered with all
that money and judgment can obtain in the shape of
tackle and rod, at the same time hoping that his gar-
ments are composed of those sober quiet colors that
are least observable; for whether in shooting, deer-
stalking, or fishing, attention to this is all important;
that he wears naught that is not useful, and not like
the Laocoon, as I once observed a young gentleman,
so covered was he with straps and bright-colored
strings suspending lunch-box, and flasks, and innumerable other contrivances, the very weight of which
must have impeded his movements and fagged him
to death long ere the day was over. He is on the

river's margin, at a spot free from bush, rock, or other impediment. The rod is carefully put together (I hope it is a spliced one, for I shall have more hope for the beginner's ultimate success from this choice), the reel is attached, the line drawn through the rings, and the cast and flies carefully taken off his hat, round which they have been wrapped (to make them more subservient and less obstreperous on commencing work), and made fast to the line. Ere an attempt at the first cast is made, take one word of advice. Englishmen are so horsey in their proclivities that they invariably consider a rod, when first they handle it, an instrument to be treated and used in exactly the same manner as a carriage whip. From boyhood upward they have been used to the latter, and the Englishman's hand has obtained wonderful cunning in cracking the same. Now the two motions are essentially different; the one is performed by the quickest possible jerk, the other by making the widest possible sweep, as free from angles as the turns on a race-course. Get this information so grafted into your brain that you will not be likely to forget yourself, for on each occasion of this forgetfulness you will pay a penalty by being minus a fly, probably the trail one. I have known some persons so skilled in snapping off flies, even although possessed of considerable experience, that their custom must have been of no small advantage to the tradesman who supplied them with tackle.

Supposing the angler is facing a river which he is desirous of throwing across. The rod being held in the right hand, gradually, but with increasing velocity, raise your rod from left to right; when the line is straight out from you, make a sweep, and bring the flies down upon the water with a half-circular motion of the hand. This last movement will raise the slack of the line and cause the trail fly to strike the water first, which should always happen. When this first lesson is thoroughly learned with the left hand, it should then be practiced up and down stream: when, with perseverance and attention, such precision may be gained that the fisherman can place the flies at every effort within an inch or two of the desired spot.

STRONG SHOOTING.

Do guns of this day shoot better than those manu-factured ten years ago? The reason why I propound such a question is, that I hear and read of birds being killed steadily at seventy and eighty yards, of trap-shooting being practiced with a fifty yards' rise, and the performers scoring four out of five. I never lived in a neighborhood where it was not reported that there was a wonderful shooting gun, but I never have had the fortune to see any of them perform their unprecedented feats; either the shooter's nerves were out of order or the powder was bad. How unfortu-nate it is that powder will so often be bad, more especially when it is desirable that it should be ex-cellent. When I hear sportsmen, particularly the young gentlemen, narrate the performances of their double barrels, I can not help commiserating myself that I have never been able to obtain better than a third-rate article for my use, for I have heretofore thought the gun which killed reliably at forty and with considerable certainty at fifty yards was as near perfection as obtainable. I do not mean to say that occasionally a snipe, or even a duck, has not been turned over at seventy yards, still at such ranges I have always thought the odds very much in favor of the birds. As none of my old battery can accomplish more than above stated, before I go abroad again it would be desirable to obtain a modern gun, yet I should not like to adopt a new favorite, which would shelve an old, without first seeing him perform, but if the novice will kill steadily at seventy with ordinary gunpowder, such as Curtis and Harvey's, I shall not have a moment's hesitation on the subject; therefore I ask, do modern guns shoot much better—say thirty per cent. better—than those turned out ten years ago?

IDEAS ON DOG BREAKING.

How many that would have turned out good men and useful members of the community, have been ruined in their youth through not being understood, and possibly treated with undue severity? How many promising colts, perfect in general appearance, have turned out runaways, apt to shy, and possessed of every failing that it was possible for horseflesh to learn, therefore irrecoverably ruined, through the bullying and barbarity of the trainer? As men are ruined, as colts are ruined, so are a preponderating percentage of our pointers and setters. My old Dominie used habitu ally to go about with the end of his strap hanging out of his pocket; no ordinary strap, but what the reader might imagine a couple of feet cut off an omnibus trace, terrible only to behold by such as were fond of toffey, or encased in tight-fitting jackets. And then the possessor of this strap was no puny bookworm—no, not he—but a stalwart Celt with a biceps so tremendous that his wife, proud of his manly development, used frequently to ask her friends, her female ones of course, when discussing the relative merits of husbands, " Have you ever seen William's muscle ? " I don't know that I ever saw it ; I am certain that I often felt it, and believe now that I would have been much better informed, and at that period more devoted to my books, but for the whackings that no excuse, whether just or not, could save me from. So it is with the majority of dog-breakers, they invest their surplus cash in the purchase of the most formidable whip that can be found, and with it conspicuously displayed from the yawning pocket of their velveteen coat strut about in conscious pride, and are at once dubbed dog-breakers ; and truly they are dog breakers, if breaking the heart and spirit of poor canines deserves the appellation.

The dog I have found much like the child ; study his character, mark his eccentricities ; when he does wrong gently admonish him, when he does well, withhold not the approbation merited. Of course in both races a headstrong pupil will occasionally be found, when castigation becomes necessary. With this I can find no fault, but I am persuaded that unnecessary correction is too often administered to both. In the course of my life I have possessed a great number of pointers and setters, the majority of which I have broken, and not giving myself undeserved praise, I have had among the number dogs which I have seldom seen equaled, never surpassed, and why? Simply because I through kindness got my pupils to love me, to repose confidence in me, and never caused them to suppose that their love was misplaced and their confidence trespassed upon. No, no, neither is the strap the necessary adjunct of the schoolmaster, nor the dog-whip that of the instructor of the devoted, unselfish, enduring, and persevering companion of man. The dog, like the child, is possessed of affection, which can easily be won if the proper means are used, and affection alone will induce both child and dog to do all in their power to serve the object of their adoration.

Probably the most important point to be attended to is that the material you go to work on be well bred and well made. In a puppy two or three months old the latter is no easy thing to tell, for it is really extraordinary how they change; but if, on the other hand, he should be nine or ten months, and possessed of the following points, you may go to work with the prospect of your labor not being thrown away: Medium size, short back, strong couplings, and well ribbed up, feet and limbs large, eyes high and intelligent. This last is perhaps not so absolutely necessary, for I have seen dogs with the most washy-looking daylights possessed of wonderful sagacity, particularly among spaniels and French poodles, but I can not consider it other than a great defect in their personal appearance. Above all things, avoid a youngster with a curly tail. I know nothing more unsightly. The last, although the most requisite, desideratum is to know that the pupil possesses a good nose. When very young this is not so easy to find out, still with attention to the rapidity with which he notices tidbits of bread or meat, a probably correct opinion may be come at; but when of maturer age, say old enough to be shown game, if when hunting he carries his head well up there can be no longer room for doubt that his olfactory nerves are all right.

Your field language should always be the same, and each command be expressed by a word of one syllable, the words being as dissimilar in intonation as possible; but it is better far to do without the voice by substituting the whistle. At all events never speak to your dog while hunting unless absolutely necessary. In early education I always accompany each order with a movement of the hand; for instance, in saying "down" I hold up my right hand. In a short time the holding up the hand alone is sufficient. In quartering your ground, if your dog is far ahead and you wish him to hunt either to the right or left of his present position, with one note on the whistle attract his attention, then turn in the line you wish him to hunt, at the same time waving your hand in the desired direction. Before long, with a note on the whistle to make him look toward you, a wave of the hand will be all that is necessary to cause him to alter his course to that which may be wished.

All well-bred dogs will stand game. I believe they do it for the purpose of ascertaining the exact position of the birds, that by a sudden direct rush they may have a chance of capturing one. To prolong this pause is the important part of the youngster's education, and for that purpose the checkstring is to be used. A plan that I have adopted with the greatest success is the following :—Procure some game birds, I generally use quail, pluck the feathers from one wing so as to reduce their power of flight; drop them at different places in a grass field, marking within a few feet of the spot with a piece of paper, then give the birds ten or fifteen minutes' lair, so that they may get over their fright and move about.

Time being up, take your pupil, with check-string made fast to him, and hunt him up wind. As you approach where a bird has been deposited, caution him, appear to be anxiously expecting game, your manner will make him doubly cautious, so that when he winds the game he will give you credit for more capability of finding than himself; your ability will be appreciated, which will be shown by the desire he will manifest in carrying out your future orders; but having come up to the birds, when the dog stands tighten the check-line, bearing heavily against him if he appears determined to be headstrong, cautioning him in a soothing, confidential tone, and the instant the bird flutters up give him a sharp jerk and cause him to "down," as if the departure of the bird was his fault. Three lessons of this kind, given with care and proper attention, the pupil being at the proper stage in other respects, I have always found sufficient to make him steady on his point.

Why I disapprove so much the use of the voice, is founded on two reasons: first, that it is more alarming to game and more apt to cause them to be wild than any other sound, not even excepting the report of the gun; secondly, if you keep constantly speaking to your dogs, from hearing incessantly your voice they become so used to it, that in emergencies they will fail to give it that prompt attention so desirable. I always teach my setters and pointers to retrieve both by land and water; with the former breed this portion of their education I have never had any difficulty to impart, with the latter I have in one or two instances found a most decided antipathy to the aquatic portion, yet I have always succeeded in the end by following this plan. When the weather is warm take the youngsters with you bathing, with one or two more aged and previously instructed companions, wade some distance out and then call them; if you have gained their affection they will ultimately come; if you can do so without alarming them caress them when in the water, and give them a small piece of food. After getting the puppies to wade till nearly out of their depth, cross deeper water, and if they will not come at first, hide yourself, occasionally calling them; I never knew an instance in which they would not ultimately come, more particularly when they see the example of their more aged companions. A few lessons of this sort will give them confidence, and after instructing them to retrieve by land, they will do the same from water.

Some dogs have a natural tendency to retrieve; with such there will be no difficulty, while others take a long time to comprehend what is desired of them, one pupil that I possessed coud not be tempted for a length of time to take any thing in his mouth and carry it. For days I tried to overcome this repugnance till my patience was almost exhausted; at last I adopted a new plan and found it successful. I attached a long string to a ball and after rolling it from me, he would go and nose it, but do no more; when he was about to leave, by pulling the ball his curiosity became excited, and he would then lay hold of it. Repeating this, it awakened a desire to retain it, and at length, as if in sheer opposition, he would keep it in his mouth and carry it with him. With others I have tried the same course, and always successfully. I do not consider any dog of these breeds perfectly broken that will not retrieve from both elements ; and although I know that in England it is not generally considered a necessary part of their education, the advantages are so obvious that it does not need further comment. At four or five months old you should commence to handle your youngsters. Accustom them to the roads, it will help to overcome their timidity and assist in hardening their feet. At six or seven months they should be familiar and conversant with the more simple portions of their education, such as " down," " heel,"&c.; and at about ten months game can be shown them; but on no account permit them to do a day's work, or exhaust themselves in hunting, till six or seven months more are over their heads. As to speed, it is a common supposition that if a dog have a good nose he can not have too much speed; but very fast dogs are apt to run over game, and consequently flush it from the very rate they are moving at. I have observed also that those who will do the longest and severest day's work are less impetuous as a rule than others. When shooting regularly, the dogs in use should always be kept in their kennel except when in the field; their associating liberty with their work makes them more zealous and anxious to please. On hunting days one good substantial meal, immediately after reaching home, with a piece of oaten or coarse bread in the middle of the day, will be found the best working diet; a dog with a full stomach is in a most unfit state to be used.

There is one description of dog I never would keep in my kennel, viz., one that trails his game. Some

persons recommend an artifice to make him hold his
head up, which is in my opinion all nonsense, because the fault lies in the animal being defective in
scenting powers.   But even if such should not be the
case, and they are capable of finding as much game
as the dog who ranges with his head up, you will not
have the same sport, for although game may lie well
to the latter, they certainly will not to the former.
The birds possibly argue thus, "that harum-scarum
fellow with head up, slashing along after some important business to the other side of the field, is too pre-
occupied to mind us; as long as we lie close, there is
nothing to be feared."   But, on the other hand, the
inquiry (if birds talk to one another) will be made by
some sagacious old paterfamilias, "What's that pottering dog doing down there?"   All eyes are immediately directed to the disagreeable intruder in
question, and very soon it becomes a decided point
among the feathered family that their footsteps are
being followed, and that with felonious intentions,
and in preference to waiting for further information
they wing their way to safer retreats.   It is not
because birds and quadrupeds don't talk that
they don't think, particularly wild ones, when it is
on a point regarding safety.   When young dogs are

so jealous and headstrong that they will not back one another, it is well to use them separately, along with an old and stanch favorite. A point being obtained by the senior, let the younger approach him as close as, if possible, for him to see the old dog, then make him down charge, by raising your hand, and keep him in that position till your barrels are reloaded; but if it be attainable, the elder dog being the farthest ahead, call up the pupil and give him the wind, afterward slowly approaching where the first point is made, showing by both manner and voice that you are on the *qui vive*, and do not let his pace be faster than your own till the elder dog is reached, when any attempt to outstrip or go ahead of the proprietor of the find, should be instantly corrected. With a little patience and repetition of these maneuvers success will be the result. I can not recommend, however, the practice of constantly hunting old and young dogs together; for the former, from greater experience, will find more game, and the latter seeing this will begin to disbelieve in his own powers, and follow the veteran, that he may always be at hand when sport is obtained.

The report of the gun should invariably be the signal for dogs to drop to shot; this lesson should early

be inculcated at home. To familiarize the dog with
the gun I have been in the habit of taking a pistol
with me to the kennel, and all the youngsters being
called into the yard, fire it, making all drop to shot;
after having kept them a sufficient time down, I
would cause the food to be brought in, and with a
wave of the hand permit them to rise and have their
grub. To have to shout "down," keeping an eye at
the same time on each of your dogs so as to enforce
the order if necessary, is very unsportsmanlike, and
certainly very much out of place when all your
powers of vision and observation are indispensable
to mark where the departing covey are going to
pitch, or the dead and wounded drop.

When seeking for a wounded or killed bird never
allow your dogs to know that you have been unsuccessful : if you have given as long a time as you can
spare for the purpose and see no ultimate prospect of
finding, take one of your bagged birds and drop it
when the dog is engaged, then cast back that he may
wind it, and thus believe that his search has not been
fruitless.

The setters most in vogue at the present day I do
not like nearly as much as those that were preferred
fifteen years ago, for this reason, that they appear to

12

me too seedy; such of **course may** suit the person
who only shoots **a few hours at a time, and then**
over highly cultivated level land, but the sportsman
who goes in for work, who shoots for shooting's sake,
and not simply to get up an appetite, to whom every
day that he is out is too short, would, I am certain,
find more satisfaction in the representatives of the old
school. Some time since so deeply was I impressed
with this idea, that I crossed some of my stock with
a well-bred, but rather large cover spaniel; the result
was that the second cross were not only handsome,
but animals that there was no end of work in, with
great activity and energy.

It frequently happens that among a lot of youngsters you will find one most provokingly backward,
who won't hunt or take any interest in the proceed-
ings. Put a curb on your temper and have patience.
You may have to wait, but gradually the apathy will
wear off, and ultimately he may turn out the flower
of the flock. I remember a youngster, which until he
was eighteen months old, refused to take notice of
game. Two or three times a week, for months, he
saw birds killed, yet all was incapable of imbuing him
with the proper spirit, for he would scarcely ever leave
heel. At length the ice was broken. He got by ac-

cident among a covey, which his experience told him he would flush if he moved, and from that day a new era commenced in his life. But this is not so much to be wondered at. Can not all of us remember some contemporaries at school who were supposed to be almost wanting common sense, but who, ultimately, turned out brilliant men? Intellect is not equally rapidly developed in each, and precocity is not always the precursor of brilliancy in mature life.

Having said thus much about our favorites, I can scarcely lay down my pen without expressing an idea or two on the lords of the creation. Bad sportsmen never have good dogs. The fussy, nervous, excitable person never has good dogs. It is a moral impossibility that they can be so, although they may have been most perfectly broken. In such hands they are certain to retrograde in performance, in the same way that the regiment that is perfect in its drill when under its cool and collected colonel, becomes a rabble under the irate, irascible, nervous major. " Keep cool" should be your motto; for if you can not, your success will only be moderate. Nothing is so destructive to both dogs and success as hurry. Listen in conclusion to the advice of an old and excellent sportsman, and you will see that his ideas much coin-

cide with mine :—Above all things never permit yourself to be hurried; but when using youngsters, yes,
and even old and tried dogs, perform your loading
and duties with as much accuracy as a soldier upon
parade, remembering that the loss of a crippled bird
is nothing to spoiling a valuable dog; for those which
have courage and energy, and consequently the most
promising, will, from such neglect, be the most liable
to suffer.

WILDERNESS LIFE.

Circumstances had caused me to attach myself to a trader, who, with about twenty teamsters, was *en route* for northern Mexico. My duties were to hunt and supply the party with game, a pleasant enough occupation but not without danger, for the greater portion of the country we traversed belonged to the much-dreaded Comanche, the most reckless race of freebooters and horsemen probably on the face of the earth, who are at war with every one, and prize nothing more than a white man's scalp. Knowing such to be the case it behooved me to keep my weather eye open when separated from my newly-formed acquaintances, but for all my watchfulness I several times had narrow escapes. Still time fled pleasantly onward, and as I write this I look back with delight to the happy, free, thoughtless hours passed either in the saddle or watching the movements of the wild animals that knew no bounds to their demesne. The Indians seldom troubled my thoughts, for I had a mare, that

I daily rode, handsome as a picture, and as game, fleet, and enduring as any animal I had ever thrown a leg over, thorough-bred I believe, and as sagacious as a dog. Between her and my bat mule there existed a most extraordinary affection. I had but to go ahead, and the latter was certain to follow, so if I did not fall into an ambuscade I knew full well I could distance any Comanche braves till I regained camp, where, behind the wagons backed by the stalwart Missourian teamsters, who well knew the use of their rifles, I would be safe. Unfortunately the principal of the expedition was a most unpleasant and unpopular person, so that between his bullying and his unpleasant manner, a mutiny was raised among his retainers, and the consequence was that the majority started *en masse* on their own hook, to seek another employer, or find their way back to their native State.

My education and antecedents had been such as to give me a horror of mutiny; moreover, up to this date, I had nothing to complain of, so I determined to stick to the wagons, and use every effort in my power to save the owner from the only alternative that appeared left, the deserting of all his property in the wilderness. Ere long, however, I was com-

pelled to change my resolution, for no one could submit to his irascible temper and constant insulting language; so, with no companions but my mare and
mule, I left the camp, one bright morning in the month
of February, with the determination of returning eastward alone. The step was full of danger, but I preferred running the risk rather than remain to be further insulted, or seek redress by recourse to weapons,
too often done in this lawless portion of the world.

As the teams were being hitched up I started in
the reverse direction, little aware of the trying ordeal
that was before me. My animals were in good condition and spirits.

For a week I traveled northeast, in the hope of
finding a suitable halting-place to remain in till
spring fairly commenced. At length I came upon
a spot which took my fancy—a small table-land
well sheltered from the northern wind, and underneath a valley, from which the snow had partially
disappeared, and where there was a fair quantity of
bunch grass, the most desirable food for the quadrupeds. Under a projecting rock I made my camp,
for the spot was so inclosed that I hoped the light-
ing of a fire would not attract attention. Weeks
rolled by, and the mare and mule lost little of their

condition, although the weather was frequently pinching cold. The cañons in the neighborhood supplied me with abundance of game, and each day I
expected that a break in the weather would justify a
start for the eastern settlements. Of course one day
was only in outline a repetition of the other, but how
widely different in detail. In the morning the horses
were taken to the bottom, breakfast was cooked,
the enjoyable pipe lit, and the direction settled in
which I would hunt, returning earlier or later, according to success. The afternoon would pass mending
moccasins or clothes, cleaning arms or arranging
camp, procuring firewood, till it was time to hunt up
the nags, which being accomplished, and the evening
meal dispatched, on a bed of leaves I would smoke
myself to sleep, painting pictures of distant home till
no longer conscious. A hunter's camp always becomes
a rendezvous for two or three wolves, and two of
these scoundrels were seldom beyond sight. Latterly they became so tame that they would come close
enough to pick up a bone if thrown to them, and one
night when the cold was more rigorous than usual,
on awaking to add fresh fuel to the fire, I saw one of
them sitting beside the warm embers, nodding his
head like a sleepy listener to a prosy sermon. Every

day I expected to be able to set out. The appearance of the sky denoted change as I turned in on the last evening, but whether it was anticipation of the good things to be obtained when civilization had been reached, I know not, or an unaccountable consciousness that danger was not far distant, I could not sleep. First I tried one side and then the other, but without effect. As it was not cold the fire had gradually decayed till only a few embers remained, making the surrounding darkness more intense. While I was hesitating whether the rebuilding of the fire or a fresh pipe would induce sleep, uneasiness seemed to have taken possession of my animals. The mule was as watchful as a dog, and as I knew he would not leave his friend, I invariably left him untied. Several times he uttered that short, quick snort so peculiar to the species, and always indicative of alarm, while the mare kept moving as far as her lariat would permit her. It might be any thing, from a deer to an Indian, so as my arms were at hand, I quietly crawled out of my lair, taking special caution that no momentary flicker from the fire should disclose my movements, and by a short *détour* got beside the nags, and soon had the soft, silky muzzle of Beckey in the palm of my hand. The greatest disaster a man can suffer in such a situation is the loss either of his ammunition or of his horses. If there were any hostile redskins in the neighborhood, by the step I had taken a stampede of my animals was now impossible. A few of the longest hours I thus sat, my presence reassuring the beasts, and, when day broke, so still had all become, that I doubt not I should have been asleep, only that the hour preceding day is well known to be invariably the time selected by Indians to carry out their machinations. In the morning, quietly moving about camp, as if pursuing unsuspiciously my usual avocations, I particularly examined the locality, when, among the remaining scattered patches of snow, the easily-distinguished bruised moccasin track of an Indian was discovered, doubtless made by a brave, who in search for game had got benighted, when he had stumbled across my hiding-place. My camp was therefore no longer safe; the coming night, he, with his companions, would be back, when woe betide the solitary white man. My horses I accompanied to their feeding-ground, not permitting them to get beyond control, and as soon as their appetites were sufficiently satisfied, I returned to my little home for the last time. The few trifles I possessed were soon packed, and nothing remained further to delay me. Still I waited a quarter of an hour longer, for the purpose of building a pile of wood, in which I placed some smoldering embers, in the hope that it would not blaze up till several hours after dark—an indication that I doubted not the redskins would construe into a certain evidence that I was still ignorant of being discovered. On my arrival in the Bayou my mare had been a little tender in front from her hoofs having been worn very close; the period of rest had rectified this, and, full of hope and anticipation, I pushed my way eastward, the only regret that passed like a cloud over my mind occurring as I took the last, ay, and long look, at my wilderness home.

CHOICE BOOKS FOR SPORTSMEN.

"Great in mouths of wisest censure."

I.

FRANK FORESTER'S FIELD SPORTS of the United States and British Provinces of North America. By HENRY WM. HERBERT.

New Edition, revised since the death of Mr. Herbert, containing corrections and additions, with a brief Memoir of the author. With numerous Illustrations on wood of every species of Game, drawn from Nature.
Two vols. crown 4to., tinted paper, green and scarlet cloth, gilt back and sides. $7 50

II.

FRANK FORESTER'S FISH AND FISHING of the United States and British Provinces. Illustrated from Nature by One Hundred Engravings on Wood, and a Steel Plate of Twenty-four Colored Flies. By HENRY WM. HERBERT.

This Edition has been thoroughly revised since the death of Mr. Herbert, and is enlarged by the addition of a Practical Treatise on Fly Fishing, by DINKS.
One vol. crown 4to., tinted paper, green and scarlet cloth, gilt back and side.... 5 50

III.

FRANK FORESTER'S HORSE AND HORSEMANSHIP of the United States and British Provinces of North America. By HENRY WM. HERBERT.

Illustrated with steel-engraved Original Portraits, from paintings and drawings, by the most distinguished artists, of celebrated Horses, including numerous fine wood engravings. New Revised Edition.
Two vols. imperial 8vo., embossed cloth, gilt back and side................. 20 00

IV.

FRANK FORESTER'S COMPLETE MANUAL for Young Sportsmen, of Fowling, Fishing, and Field Sports.

With directions for handling the Gun, the Rifle, and the Rod. Illustrated with numerous Engravings on Wood. Prepared for the instruction and use of the Youth of America, by HENRY WM. HERBERT.
One vol. crown 8vo., tinted paper, green and scarlet cloth, pp. 450.......... 3 00

V.

THE DOG. By DINKS, MAYHEW, AND HUTCHINSON.—Compiled, Illustrated, and Edited by FRANK FORESTER.

Profusely Illustrated with Original Drawings. Embracing the SPORTSMAN'S VADE-MECUM, by "DINKS." DOGS: THEIR MANAGEMENT; by EDWARD MAYHEW. DOG-BREAKING: by COL. W. N. HUTCHINSON.
One vol. crown 8vo., tinted paper, green and scarlet cloth, pp. 664.......... 3 00

VI.

THE DEAD SHOT; OR, SPORTSMAN'S COMPLETE GUIDE; being a Treatise on the use of the Gun, with rudimentary and finishing lessons in the Art of Shooting Game of all kinds : Pigeon-Shooting, Dog-Breaking, etc. By MARKSMAN.

With six full page Engravings of Attitudes and Positions. With explanations of the diff'rence and relations of English and American Game, from the works of FRANK FORESTER.
One vol. 12mo., uniform with THE CRACK SHOT............................ 2 00

Published by W. A. TOWNSEND & ADAMS, 434 Broome Street.
Mailed by the Publishers free of Postage, and for sale by all Booksellers.

CRITICAL OPINIONS OF THE DEAD SHOT.

"THE DEAD SHOT is in every respect the best work on the art of shooting for the young sportsman. It comprises a searching and clear exposition of the secrets of good shooting, with the best practical instructions in dog-breaking. All who read it will assuredly profit by its truthful and convincing explanations. Bad shots, nervous and inexperienced sportsmen, who peruse this little treatise, will find much light thrown on the mystery of shooting with unerring precision."—SPORTING MAGAZINE.

"MARKSMAN'S opinion is entitled to respect, because he shows in every page of his book that he understands the subject of which he treats. His advice to young sportsmen is brief, clear, and practical; and we believe that he who acts upon it steadily can not fail to improve his shooting; and if nature has given him a quick eye and steady hand and nerve he will have placed himself in the right road to attain the reputation of a dead shot."—SATURDAY REVIEW.

"THIS is the most complete sportsman's manual that we have yet seen; and we feel a pleasure in recommending it to the notice of every one who carries a gun after game, whether he be an old hand or a mere tyro. If the former, he will find much to enjoy in the record of work cleverly done, together with a profusion of useful hints that can not fail to satisfy and please; if the latter, in MARKSMAN he meets a friend who will lead him from the first rudimentary lesson in handling a gun, to the proficiency of a dead shot. We have not read a more useful or agreeable sporting book for a long time, and heartily recommend it to every sportsman, old as well as young."—BELL'S LIFE.

"THIS is a capital little book, the work of a man who thoroughly knows what he is writing about. The Volunteer movement has naturally led to the publication of several treatises on the use of a gun, especially the use of a rifle; but we do not call to mind any one that so completely comes up to our own notion of a useful manual on the science of shooting as this of MARKSMAN'S. We feel quite sure, that by a close adherence to the rules and instructions here given, the shooter can not fail to become a good shot, and will, very probably, become a dead shot."—MORNING CHRONICLE.

"MARKSMAN'S volume is worth the study of sportsmen, whether young or old. We particularly recommend to the former the attitudes represented in the plates."—GARDENERS' CHRONICLE.

"WE fully believe that the careful study of this book will be equivalent to a considerable amount of practice in fitting a man to do his work in the field with credit to himself. The author writes like a man who thoroughly understands his business. His maxims are all plain, intelligible, and founded on common sense. . . . The book is full of practical and precisely-expressed rules, which are fully supported by reason; and which, if they are carefully observed, will bring any one, with a reasonable amount of practice, steady nerves, and a good eye, up to the level implied in the phrase, 'a dead shot.'"—JOHN BULL.

"TO teach the novice how to handle a gun, and to hit with certainty, and to cure defects in bad marksmen, is the object of the DEAD SHOT. Commencing with the gun itself, MARKSMAN enters con amore upon his task, and proceeds from the A, B, C of the art to the utmost limits which the theory can reach. One of the most valuable divisions of the book is that which treats of the flight of game, a topic that has not been discussed in other works on shooting. The advantages of a knowledge of this subject to the young sportsman can not be over-rated. Directions for Dog-breaking are added, so that the DEAD SHOT is, as its title professes, the SPORTSMAN'S COMPLETE GUIDE."—MORNING POST.

THE CRACK SHOT:

Or, THE YOUNG RIFLEMAN'S COMPLETE GUIDE.

BEING A TREATISE ON THE USE OF THE RIFLE, WITH RUDIMENTARY AND FINISH
ING LESSONS, INCLUDING A FULL DESCRIPTION OF THE LATEST IMPROVED BREECH
LOADING WEAPONS, ILLUSTRATED WITH NUMEROUS ENGRAVINGS; RULES AND
REGULATIONS FOR TARGET PRACTICE; DIRECTIONS FOR HUNTING GAME FOUND IN
THE UNITED STATES AND BRITISH PROVINCES, ETC., ETC.

BY EDWARD C. BARBER.

Third Edition, now Ready.

OPINIONS OF THE LEADING JOURNALS.

" WE have read 'The Crack Shot' with care, and find it to
be a clever and thorough work, such as we expected from the talent and
conscientious pains-taking of the author, and recommend it strongly to the rifle,
shooter. . . . . . It is full of information, and is calculated to be of great use to
young beginners with the rifle, and old hands with that famous weapon will also
derive much instruction from its pages. Mr. Barber is a thorough, practical shot,
and has produced a treatise on Rifle Shooting of permanent interest and value."—
SPIRIT OF THE TIMES.

" GLADLY will the public hail this new book on the rifle, by
a practical American sportsman. It contains a full description of the latest
improved breech-loading weapons, illustrated by carefully drawn engravings, accompanied by elaborate explanations. The maxims and rules of the art of shooting
are laid down with clearness and brevity. The book is published in excellent style."
—TURF, FIELD, AND FARM.

" THE author has supplied a want which has been long much
felt. It first treats of the general principles of firing and motion of projectiles, and then on rifling, discussing the merits of the various forms of groove and
twist, and, after describing with illustrations the best American and foreign breech-
loaders, gives directions how to choose and how to use a rifle. It closes with directions for hunting the various kinds of game. We commend it heartily to all who
take pleasure in field sports, and those interested in military arms."—AMERICAN
ARTISAN.

" THE book must prove a valuable assistance to our young
riflemen, and a great help in teaching them how to become 'crack shots.'
The illustrations increase the worth of the book materially."—MONTREAL NEWS.

" FOR those who are ambitious to become a 'crack shot' this
book will prove to be invaluable. The rifle in all its various forms is
fully discussed. . . . . Nothing better of the kind could be desired. It is sure to
be immensely popular with all sportsmen and those who love the rifle."—N. Y.
EVENING MAIL.

" MR. BARBER'S new sporting volume treats of the latest
improved breech-loading fire-arms; the rules and regulations of target
exercise; especial directions for hunting game, etc., with such other information as
will interest all sportsmen. The work is an able one, and fills a place hitherto un-
occupied."—CHICAGO EVENING JOURNAL.

One volume small 12mo. extra cloth, gilt back, side stamp and beveled boards, 342
pages, numerously illustrated. Price $2 50. Uniform with " THE DEAD SHOT."

Published by W. A. TOWNSEND & ADAMS, 434 Broome-st., N. Y.

Mailed by the Publishers free of postage, and for sale by all Booksellers.

HORSE PORTRAITURE.

Breeding, Rearing, and Training Trotters; Preparation for Races; Management in the Stable; On the Track; Horse Life, &c., &c.

BY JOSEPH CAIRN SIMPSON.

New Edition, With Index.

One crown 8vo volume, tinted paper, beveled boards, green and scarlet cloth, gilt back and sides. Uniform with "COMPLETE MANUAL FOR YOUNG SPORTSMEN."

Price, $3 00

Published by W. A. TOWNSEND & ADAMS, 434 Broome-st., N. Y.

Mailed by the Publishers free of postage, and for sale by all Booksellers.

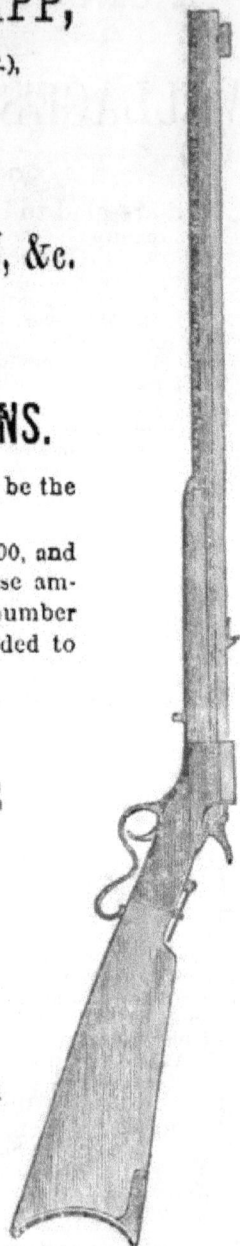

Books for Sportsmen and Agriculturists,

PUBLISHED BY

GEORGE ROUTLEDGE & SONS,

416 Broome Street, New York.

THE HORSE IN THE STABLE AND THE FIELD. His varieties: Management in Health and Disease; Anatomy; Physiology, &c. By STONE-HENGE. Illustrated with 170 engravings by Barraud, Weir, Zwecker, and others. 8vo.

A New Edition, with on Appendix by Alfred Large M. D., M. R. C. V. S. L., and Professor at the New York College of Veterinary Surgeons. 8vo. cloth $5.00.

" So far as authority goes, we need hardly say that this book is entitled to the first rank...... We know of no treatise on the noble animal more worthy of attention than this."—*Boston Daily Advertiser.*

STONEHENGE'S SHOT-GUN AND SPORTING RIFLE. A complete Compendium for Sports wherein the Gun or Rifle is used, with full descriptions of the Dogs, Ponies, Ferrets, &c., used in the various kinds of Shooting and Trapping. Illustrated with 20 large page engravings and 100 wood-cuts. Post, 8vo., half-bound, $5.00.

Pages 163 to 290 of this excellent manual are devoted to descriptions of the various guns and rifles of the most celebrated makers, and contain upwards of 60 engravings of different descriptions of guns and rifles, both breech and muzzle-loading.

☞ THE RIFLE AND HOW TO USE IT Containing a description of that valuable weapon in all its varieties. By Hans Busk, author of " Navies of the World," " Rifle Volunteers," &c. Eighth Edition, considerably enlarged and improved. Illustrated with numerous wood engravings and portraits. F'cap, 8vo., half-bound, $1.25.

THE POULTRY BOOK. Comprising the Breeding and Management of Profitable and Ornamental Poultry, and their qualities and characteristics. By W. B. TEGETMEIER. With 50 full page colored illustrations and numerous wood engravings. Royal 8vo. Cloth, $9.00.

"Mr. Tegetmeier has certainly succeeded in producing a work which not only excels any we have met with on the subject, but one which must, from its comprehensive character, long remain the standard book of instruction and reference to all poultry fanciers."—*Round Table.*

PIGEONS. Their structure, varieties, habits, and management. By W. B. TEGETMEIER, author of " The Poultry Book." Illustrated with many beautifully colored representations of the different varieties, drawn from life by Harrison Weir. Royal 8vo. Cloth, $5.00.

"The editor has endeavored to produce a treatise that shall furnish the amateur of Pigeons with a greater amount of practical information than is to be found in any previous volume."—*From the Preface.*

FRANCIS ON FISH CULTURE, and the modern system of breeding and rearing fish in inland waters, containing numerous illustrations. Post, 8vo. Cloth, $2.00.

HOW TO FARM PROFITABLY; or the Sayings and Doings of Mr. Alderman Mechi. With a portrait, and illustrations from photographs by Mayall. A new and enlarged Edition. F'cap, 8vo., half-bound, $2.50.

In this Edition are included Mr. Mechi's valuable pamphlets on Town Sewerage and Steam Ploughing.

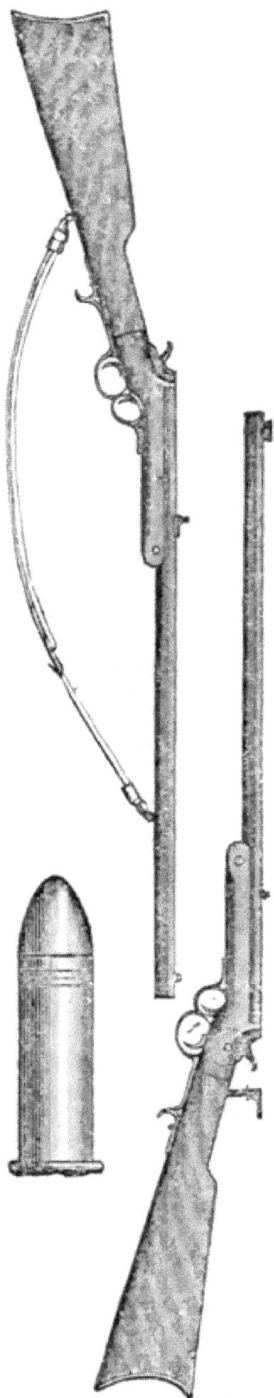

FUR, FIN, AND FEATHER:

CONTAINING THE

GAME LAWS

OF THE PRINCIPAL STATES OF THE

UNITED STATES AND CANADA.

Price, in Paper Covers, 50 Cts.; Cloth, $1.50.

RULES AND REGULATIONS

FOR THE GOVERNMENT OF

RACING, TROTTING, AND BETTING,

REVISED AND CORRECTED.

TO WHICH IS ADDED NUMEROUS DECISIONS ON DISPUTED TURF
MATTERS, COMPILED FROM THE "ANSWERS TO COR-
RESPONDENTS," AS GIVEN IN "WILKES' SPIRIT
OF THE TIMES," THE RECOGNIZED AU-
THORITY ON ALL SPORTING TOPICS
IN AMERICA.

PRICE:

Paper Covers, $1.50; Boards, $2; Cloth, $2.50.

☞ Mailed free of Postage on Receipt of Price, by

M. B. BROWN & CO.,
99 & 101 William Street.

MARTIN B. BROWN. }
CHARLES SUYDAM. }

M. B. BROWN & CO., Commercial Printers, Stationers, Blank Book Manu-
facturers, Lithographers, Engravers, &c., 99 & 101 William Street, near John,
New York.

www.ingramcontent.com/pod-product-compliance
Lightning Source LLC
Chambersburg PA
CBHW020513270326
41926CB00008B/855